PUBLICATIONS OF THE FACULTY OF ARTS
OF THE UNIVERSITY OF MANCHESTER

No. 20

PLATO'S *SOPHIST*

PLATO'S *SOPHIST*

A commentary by
RICHARD S. BLUCK

Edited by
GORDON C. NEAL

MANCHESTER
UNIVERSITY PRESS

© 1975 University of Manchester

Published by the University of Manchester at
THE UNIVERSITY PRESS
Oxford Road, Manchester M13 9PL

ISBN 0 7190 1271 6

184
PT150-x&

76-3910
Printed in Great Britain by
Western Printing Services Ltd, Bristol

CONTENTS

AUTHOR'S FOREWORD

The problems raised by the *Parmenides* being extremely complicated, and the date of the *Timaeus* being a matter of dispute, studying the *Sophist* is perhaps the most promising way of trying to discover whether, and if so in what manner, Plato's philosophy—and in particular his theory of Forms—developed or changed after the writing of the *Republic*. But even the *Sophist* has been read in radically different ways. Some scholars hold that the 'Greatest Kinds' (μέγιστα γένη or εἴδη) discussed in the *Sophist* are not meant to be interpreted as Platonic Forms, and their arguments have not perhaps been given sufficient attention. Those, on the other hand, who have assumed that the Kinds can be taken as Forms, or 'are' Forms—whether of the *Republic* type or not—have often levelled very just criticism against existing explanations of particular passages made on the same assumption, but have themselves substituted explanations that are in fact no less implausible; and the difficulties thus revealed might seem to support the view that the Eleatic Visitor is not expounding Platonic doctrine but engaging very largely in sophistical arguments, albeit with (perhaps) the enlightened aim of exposing sophistry.

No doubt the dialogue is capable, and is meant to be capable, of being interpreted without reference to Platonic Forms. The arguments of the unconverted sophist against the possibility of saying or thinking what is false must be controverted with arguments that he will accept as valid. Yet at the same time it is most unlikely that Plato would repeatedly use the term εἴδη without bearing in mind that readers acquainted with his earlier works would at once think of his Forms; and it is therefore highly probable that what is said is meant to be capable of being interpreted in terms of Forms. This is all the more likely, as a great deal is said about one Kind (γένος) or Form (εἶδος) partaking of another, and the question was raised in the *Parmenides*, clearly with reference to the theory of Forms, whether one εἶδος could partake of another. It is therefore a reasonable working hypothesis that the arguments are intended to be interpreted in terms of Platonic Forms by those acquainted with Platonic doctrine, while at the same time being capable of being interpreted without special reference to such doctrine by those who rejected it or had no knowledge of it. The aim in what follows is to try to determine the most natural significance of each argument from the Platonist's point of view, taking the γένη or εἴδη as Forms, and to see whether these arguments and the dialogue as a whole will, after all, make good sense when so interpreted. A positive answer to this question will emerge as the book proceeds. The reader must judge whether the case is proved.

Those who have never doubted that the Kinds can be taken as Forms may consider such an enquiry unnecessary. But there are many passages, as has already been mentioned, where difficulties raised have never been satisfactorily met, and the precise nature of the Platonic doctrine implied is still far from clear. New interpretations are here offered, for example, of the arguments for the separateness of the Kinds (chapter VII), of what is meant by a vowel Form (chapter VI), and of the argument against the monists (chapter III).

Although the commentary is grounded at every point

in the Greek text of the *Sophist*, the discussion is presented through the medium of translation for the benefit of Greekless readers. Certain crucial terms or phrases are quoted in Greek but always with at least a provisional English rendering alongside. The aim is to make some of the more substantive linguistic issues accessible in spite of the limitations of translation. In particular, the attempt is made to indicate faithfully Plato's use of certain more technical terms which have no single English equivalent and are therefore normally rendered in translation in a variety of ways in different contexts (thus pre-empting consideration of important points of interpretation). Some textual and grammatical questions of Greek are referred to in the notes, but these are not essential to the main argument of the book.

University of Manchester
September 1963   RICHARD S. BLUCK

EDITOR'S FOREWORD

When Richard Bluck died suddenly of a coronary throm-
bosis eleven years ago, in September 1963, he left the
manuscript of a commentary on Plato's *Sophist* three-
quarters complete. It is perhaps the greatest possible
tribute to his scholarship that in spite of the enormous
torrent of work on the *Sophist* that the intervening decade
has seen published, Bluck's interpretation, on both the
large and the small scale, is still relevant. And by courtesy
of Manchester University Press, and in particular the
Arts Faculty editorial board, it is fortunately possible to
give it now the public it deserves.

No attempt has been made to supply the missing final
chapter or two. The completed chapters are in the
nature of a running commentary, self-contained as far
as they go and by a happy chance stopping at one of the
main structural divisions of the *Sophist* (259d). Bluck
appears to have tackled the dialogue section by section,
completing each chapter before moving on to the next.
Certainly no notes were found anywhere among his
papers which gave any indication of how he would have
tackled the remaining pages, except for the draft of an
article intended as a reply to Peck's criticisms (*Phronesis*,
1962) of Bluck's earlier discussion of false statement in
JHS, 1957. Even here there was nothing like a systematic
exposition of the text, and apparently no change of view
since the 1957 article. The bulk of the material in the
draft concerned earlier sections of the dialogue, and had
been superseded by the present commentary.

As editor, I have tried to do two things. In the first

place, indexes, bibliography, and many of the references had to be supplied, some obscurities of exposition in Bluck's MS removed, and the last few pages of chapter VIII reconstructed. Beyond this I have made a few additions of my own. These consist of a short bio-graphical tribute to the author, an introductory sketch (with some critical comments of my own) of some of the most important work on the *Sophist* published since Bluck wrote, and in the notes, references and comments relating to detailed points where recent writers impinge most closely on Bluck's argument (these last all identified by square brackets).

I am happy to be able to record here my gratitude for help of many kinds offered to me at various stages of the editing of this book. As always, much of this assistance will remain unrecognized and unacknowledged, as un-fortunately also must any debts which Bluck would have wished to confess. I know only that members of the Northern, Scottish and Southern Associations for Ancient Philosophy heard and discussed with Bluck earlier drafts of certain chapters. For myself, my thanks go particularly to Mr Alex Adamson, Mr John Banks, Mr Brendan Darcy, Mr E. J. Kenney, Professor G. B. Kerford, Mrs Eileen Neal, Mrs Mabel Neal, and Professor H. D. Westlake.

University of Manchester   GORDON NEAL
July 1974

BIOGRAPHICAL NOTE

Richard Bluck died on 29 September 1963 at the age of 44. He had published four books, twenty-four articles and innumerable reviews. He was promoted Reader at Manchester twelve months before his death, and received an Edinburgh D.Litt. for published work in 1961. The man who F. M. Cornford had reportedly asserted should never have been allowed to do Greek philosophy had made his mark in his chosen field and was aiming (surely realistically) at a Chair.

He had, however, been under the doctor for some years because of a heart condition, although none of his colleagues was really aware of this. So the massive coronary from which he died almost instantly was to them as totally unexpected as it was a sad curtailment at the peak of his career.

The four years he spent in the Department of Greek at Manchester, to which he came as Senior Lecturer in 1959, were particularly productive. They saw the publication of his major work, a full-scale edition of Plato's *Meno*, the preparation of the present commentary on the *Sophist*, and also the appearance of at least ten articles in professional journals.

He was a dedicated, thorough scholar. In Greek philosophy his overriding interest was in the task of interpreting Plato as a creature of his own times and not, as Bluck felt was too often done in some quarters, as a kind of modern logician *manqué*. Of the *Meno* edition, Professor G. B. Kerferd wrote in a review (*CR*, 1963, p. 43), 'It provides materials for bringing together the

philosophical and the philological study of Plato in a
way that is very desirable.' Professor J. B. Skemp had
earlier commented (*CR*, 1951, p. 86) on the contribution
made to the interpretation of Plato in historical context
by Bluck's first two books, *Plato's Seventh and Eighth
Letters* (Cambridge, 1947) and *Plato's Life and Thought*
(London, 1949). From another wing of Platonic studies
Renford Bambrough gave this assessment of Bluck's
Meno in *JHS*, 1964, p. 191: 'This edition is an excellent
representative of the classical tradition of sympathetic
historical interpretation of Plato, but it is also typical of
that tradition's habit of crossing from scholarship into
substantive philosophy without notice and therefore without due argument for its implicit philosophical theses.'
Bluck would have enjoyed equally, I am sure, both the
compliment and the implied criticism.

He did for the *Meno* what Dodds had done a couple of
years before for the *Gorgias*. Professor K. Gaiser credited
Bluck (*Gymnasium*, 1963, p. 440) with having provided
the first satisfactory textual *apparatus*. The scholarship of
the commentary was also widely appreciated. It was
described by Gaiser as a foundation which would be
gratefully used by all future workers in the field, an
opinion echoed by Bambrough in quizzical vein: 'Bluck
is not one of those editors who write about everything
except what is important and difficult: he writes about
everything.' If this was the fruits of the traditional ortho-
doxy of which Bluck was occasionally accused, it was
surely a fault to be proud of.

Bluck's interest in his subject did not exclude an
unobtrusively genuine concern for people. He was
anxious to teach effectively and played his part in producing materials for the job, specifically the collections

of *Greek Unseens* and *Latin Unseens* published by Manchester University Press in 1962 and 1963 respectively. He was a residential tutor in Hulme Hall throughout his time in Manchester. And—more surprisingly, because Bluck rarely talked about it—he took an active part in organizing boxing in a local boys' club. The benign, reserved, pipe-smoking philosopher did not despise the competitive life after all!

He had turned first, of course, to schoolteaching after leaving Peterhouse in 1942. He taught for ten years in a number of schools, including Marlborough and Fettes College: during his four years at the latter he obtained his Ph.D. from Edinburgh University and published two books. A year as Director of the British Council Centre in Naples preceded his belated entry into university teaching in 1953 as Assistant Lecturer at Queen Mary College, London, where he remained (as Lecturer from 1954) until he moved to Manchester.

EDITOR'S INTRODUCTION

I. THE ATTEMPT TO AVOID ANACHRONISM

It is understandable that scholars have usually interpreted the *Sophist* as an exploration of the verb 'to be'. Distinguishing this verb's various senses is vital to clear, logical thinking, and the triple analysis of identity, existence, and predication has often seemed self-evident to modern ears. Plato was clearly attempting to resolve some of the confusions of the sophists and Presocratics in this area of thought. And in assessing the value of his contribution, it is perfectly reasonable to use current views as criterion. A twentieth-century student of Plato cannot claim to understand without being able to relate what Plato says to his own view of things.

The dangers of distortion that inhere in this approach, however, are obvious. Aristotle's discussion of his predecessors, where the time gap is negligible by comparison, is a salutary caution. For the current situation with respect to the *Sophist* Kamlah's comment (40) is to the point (I translate): 'Here too the difficulty of interpretation consists in the fact that the contemporary commentator cannot always deny himself refinements and distinctions which Plato either does not draw at all or does not draw explicitly.'

To some extent the dangers can be avoided. Much recent work on the dialogue appears to have been motivated by such a desire. Ackrill's claim that Plato distinguished all three of the major senses of 'is' has seemed too simplistic an attribution of modern insights to a Greek philosopher, although he demonstrated satisfactorily that the statements that occur and are subjected to analysis in the *Sophist* include statements which we would classify under each of these three heads. Plato deserves at least the credit for a good intuitive selection of examples. And Ackrill's analysis by hindsight, as it may be termed, has been a powerful stimulus to research.

Writers since Ackrill have tried to shake free from the more obvious distortions of hindsight. Accepting for the most part that Plato was making a distinction between senses of the verb 'to be', they have tried to locate that distinction more precisely within the outlines of Plato's own conceptual map. Here, then, is the twofold task of current study, to be faithful to Plato's understanding of the problem and at the same time to relate that understanding in some meaningful way to our own conceptual framework. Although this definition of the problem is still vague, it indicates well enough how complex the task is and how it will almost inevitably require the forging of new conceptual tools—neither those in common use in Plato's time nor those of our own—if it is to be successfully accomplished.

Hence, for example, Runciman's concept (96) 'total predication and identity', an attempt along these lines but refuted by Bluck in this book. Hence too Bluck's own interpretation of the dialogue as marking off the identitative 'is' from other senses but as failing to draw any distinction between existential and predicative uses— an interpretation which links closely to the paradigm-case view of the Forms which he establishes. In much the same spirit, Cornford had earlier seen in the *Sophist* no mention of the copula at all, but a distinction between 'is' meaning 'exists' and an identitative sense which he defines widely enough to include the relationship between generic and specific Forms implied in a definition. 'A definition', he writes (296), 'is a statement of complete identity: "Man is (the same as) rational biped Animal".'

These by no means exhaust the list. I discuss Frede and Owen in more detail in the next few pages, and others are dealt with by Bluck or mentioned in my additional notes on work published since his death. Kahn has opened up yet further possibilities with his fresh analysis of the verb 'to be' in Greek. In a tantalizingly sketchy article, he argues for three basic meanings—veridical, durative, and locative–existential—which could well have relevance for Plato. We can only hope that he will apply his analysis in detail to the *Sophist* (*inter alia*) in his book on the subject, announced but not yet published as I write (see Bibliography).

Marten comments pointedly (205 f.) on the general lack of agreement that plagues this aspect of Platonic scholarship. He blames both Plato's inadequacies as a 'pre-logician' (*Vorfahren der Logik*) and the inadequacies of the scholars as 'post-exponents' (*Nachverstehende*) of his ontology. Whatever the cause—and it may simply be the variety of philosophical positions and training that exists among them—there is certainly a very ample variety among the definitions which the scholars offer us of Plato's philosophical achievement in the *Sophist*.

In fact, the proliferation of explanations produced in recent years would provide an extraordinarily rich source of material for a case study in the methodology of the history of ideas. Many of the published discussions seem to prompt a prior question, even: whether ideas are objects susceptible to historical study. The bewildering range of interpretations that this one dialogue of Plato's seems to allow certainly calls into doubt our mental model of the procedure appropriate to diachronic philosophical investigation. Anachronism threatens at every turn, and never more so, it often appears, than when the attempt is being made to avoid it. General linguistics in recent generations has put severe restrictions on the historical study of language and encouraged instead synchronic analysis. It is probably time that historians of ideas developed a similar awareness of their limitations and discovered a new vocation within the general discipline of the sociology of knowledge systems. At least some general discussion is needed on method, definitions, postulates, etc., if the debate is not to degenerate into mere manipulation of meaningless terms.

2. THREE RECENT DISCUSSIONS

Leaving such larger questions on one side as inapposite, I content myself here with commenting briefly on some of the work on the *Sophist* published since Bluck wrote. This is not intended as an exhaustive sketch. I am simply concerned to indicate where these later writers impinge most closely on Bluck's approach, and to attempt some rough-and-ready assessment of them relative to what this commentary offers. I hope that my outline may help to place Bluck's work in the context of the continuing debate, and that readers not already familiar with the current issues may be stimulated to, rather than deterred from, a wish to obtain a first-hand acquaintance with these authors.

(a) *I. M. Crombie* (1962). In accordance with the plan of his two-volume exploration of Platonism, I. M. Crombie offers not a full discussion of the *Sophist*, but a treatment of certain specific problems which the dialogue raises, both metaphysical and logical (vol. II, pp. 388–422, 492–516). In the later of these sections, he examines the usage of 'is'—with somewhat ambiguous result, as he acknowledges (509 f.). He clearly accepts that Plato distinguishes predication from identity, and, to judge from the frequent appearance of 'exist' and 'existence' in his summaries of Plato's arguments, credits him with an awareness of this meaning of the verb: he also mentions (499) its use in philosophical Greek with 'the sense . . . of something like stability, ultimacy or reality'. But at the same time he makes, for example, the paradoxical admission (510) that 'Plato is not fully and explicitly conscious of the fact that he has shown that *einai* has certain special uses'. An otherwise helpful discussion, which stresses Plato's interest in negation as such (see section 3 of this introduction), is unfortunately marred by these obscurities, which stem largely, it seems, from the perennial problem of keeping Platonic and modern terminology far enough apart to avoid confusion.

The main interest of Crombie's account, however, is in the earlier section on metaphysical analysis, and specifically in the exceptionally wide-ranging attempt to relate the Platonic Forms to modern categories. Under Crombie this is a fruitful exercise which raises a number of important questions, e.g. Are the Kinds of the *Sophist* to be seen more as classes or properties? Or does Plato appreciate at all the difference between formal, 'non-limiting' concepts like existence and identity on the one hand and on the other the substantial

properties which mark one class of things off from
another?

For the most part Crombie avoids anachronism. He is
careful to note that while Plato approaches, he nevertheless falls significantly short of, for example, the distinction between formal and material properties. But
I do feel that, perhaps from a laudable concern to
contribute something new to Platonic scholarship,
he occasionally ignores the simple interpretation. The
simple, even *à propos* the *Sophist*, is not necessarily wrong!
For instance, there are, as Crombie states, special cases
of change where the change is constant; he cites (vol. II,
p. 398; cf. 406) the earth's axial rotation. But I cannot
believe that the issue in the dialogue about whether
Change can rest (see 252d, 255a, 256b) relates in any way
to this sophisticated notion of constant change. Indeed,
it is hard to see how Crombie reaches this interpretation
at all, because it has little to do with the apparent confusion between predication and identity, which, like
Bluck, he diagnoses clearly enough as the basic difficulty.
In any case, he does not approach Bluck's solution in
terms of a paradigm-case role for the Forms (for references see p. 113, n. 2).

This central feature of Bluck's interpretation of the
dialogue affords an interesting comparison with Crombie.
Bluck sees certain difficulties in the way of understanding
the Forms as fully fledged universals—in particular, the
passages where elements of self-reference are inescapable.
This leads to what is, I am sure, the well founded suggestion that Plato is working with a conception of the
Forms which combines the roles of universal and paradigm case. In other words, Plato does not pigeonhole
precisely according to the categories of modern logic.

Crombie finds a very similar problem when he tries to classify Plato. He asks 'whether the doctrine that kinds can share amounts to the doctrine that there are class inclusions, or to the doctrine that properties can themselves have properties' (vol. II, p. 402). He sees hints of both, but is aware that neither interpretation really fits. He therefore concludes that 'Plato was operating with a pictorial conception of the terms whose relations he is discussing according to which they were simple units, neither properties nor classes but something in between' (409). Such a view of the Form as a 'counter' (Crombie's term), representing now class and now property, is certainly a possible explanation of the apparent confusion (*pace* Bluck) of negative predication and statements of non-identity at 257b ff. But Bluck's paradigm-case Form has equal potential here, and the added merit of explaining the self-predication passages which Crombie does not attempt to deal with. Both agree, though, that Plato's doctrines must not be defined in alien terms.

(b) *M. Frede* (1967). Frede's general conclusions, in an important monograph on Plato's analysis of 'is' in the *Sophist*, eschew modern categories with commendable restraint. He drops any claim that Plato is distinguishing meanings of the verb at all, even the 'is' of identity. A distinction is drawn in the dialogue, he believes (29 ff.), between two applications (*Verwendungen*) of the verb, not between meanings (*Bedeutungen*); both applications are treated as copulative in function and involving 'two-place' predication. This conclusion is based on an original and careful study of 255c-d (12 ff.), which, however, some may judge as anachronistic in applying over-sharp logical distinctions to Plato's language, e.g. that between class and property just mentioned.

A strong point of Frede's thesis is that he relates the difference between these two applications of 'is' closely to Plato's ontology. In one application, 'is x' is used of the Form X itself, and therefore 'with reference to itself' (αὐτὰ καθ' αὑτά), in the second, 'is x' is used to predicate the Form X of one of its instances, be it another Form or a particular, and therefore involves 'reference to something other' besides the subject of the sentence (πρὸς ἄλλα). At 255c-d (or elsewhere) the argument gives us no warrant to believe that Plato is trying to establish two different Forms of Being, and Frede is therefore rightly reluctant to allow the claim that he is distinguishing senses of the verb either.

If he is right, and I am inclined to agree, Bluck's view that identity and predication are carefully differentiated (for references see p. 66, n. 1) must be modified. But this would not affect his general interpretation to any great extent. Plato clearly is trying to dispel, in his discussion of the most important Kinds (see ch. VII), the confusion between statements of identity and predication which underlies the apparently contradictory nature of such pairs of true statements as 'Change is not the Same' and 'Change is the same'. Frede admits (69) that instances of 'is x' in his first application amount from one point of view to identifying statements. And Plato's solution clearly involves exploring the role of the concept of identity, or at least the Form Sameness.

Frede (31 ff.) also relates his distinction to the question of the self-predication of the Forms. He claims that 'is x' in the first application, i.e. to the Form X, avoids the danger of a regress precisely because it involves true self-predication and hence allows no chink for any trace of a 'Third Man' to enter. However, this goes considerably beyond anything that is made explicit in the dialogue, and Frede offers no real argument. In any case, it is doubtful whether he is right to claim that such self-predication would indicate that Plato had given up regarding the Forms as standard instances or paradigm cases. Bluck's argument for the continued presence of this function of the Forms in the *Sophist* (for references see p. 113, n. 2) is too firmly based in a detailed exposition of the text to be shaken by Frede's disavowal.

(c) *G. E. L. Owen* (1971). One of the most recent important treatments of the area covered by Bluck in this book is G. E. L. Owen's chapter entitled 'Plato and Not-being' in the first volume of essays on Plato edited by G. Vlastos (published in 1971). Owen supports the claims advanced by Runciman, Bluck (here), Frede, and Malcolm that no separate existential sense of the verb 'to be' is marked off in the *Sophist*. Indeed, his essay apparently makes available in English on various detailed exegetical points some of the insights worked out in seminars held during the 1950s and 1960s, just as Frede's book did for German readers in 1967 (cf. Owen, 223, n. 1, and for a specific example 256 ff., where he discusses *Sophist* 255c-d from much the same angle as Frede, 12 ff.). What is not so clear is whether Owen goes beyond this widely accepted denial that the existential sense of the verb is formally differentiated from other usages. He appears (225, 248, etc.) to be concerned to show that the very concept of existence is totally irrelevant to the problems discussed in the dialogue, however difficult modern ears might find that to believe. But his disclaimer on p. 248, for example, seems to be content to accept something more like the undifferentiated existential–copulative sense which Bluck advocates (for references see p. 63 n.).

The ambiguity in Owen's language on this point stems largely, I believe, from the general problem of interpreting historical texts in contemporary terms. Two particular issues are relevant here. Existence in modern logic is a one-place predicate, and therefore 'incomplete' uses of 'is' (whether the completion is supplied or understood) are clearly not in logic instances of the existential meaning of the verb. When Owen remarks (248) that Plato's study 'is essentially preliminary to, and not based on, the isolation or construction of the difficult notion "exist"', it is the logician's 'existence' that he has in mind, and he is no doubt right to deny this strictly understood concept to the *Sophist*. But in normal parlance we can discuss meaningfully questions about whether there is such a thing as x, whether x is anything or not, in short whether x exists, without being trained in the logical niceties. And so could the Greeks. This 'grass-roots' problem of existence, of being there or being something, can surely be said (without obscurantism and without dependence on what Owen at p. 236 ff. calls 'the reductive thesis') to underlie the issues discussed in the *Sophist*. For a similar comment see Wiggins in the same volume (271, n. 3).

The second difficulty relevant here is this. Owen and Malcolm (also Wiggins, but he seems to be more aware of the dangers of so doing) interpret the *Sophist* on the level of logic rather than metaphysics. But this too is a dangerously anachronistic distinction (cf. Meinhardt, 30 f., 71). Plato is discussing Being, not uses of '. . . is . . .'. True, he uses as evidence the semantic data of language.

But this does not make him a logician any more than it makes him an incompetent metaphysician: it is, however, evidence for the anachronism of the distinction. The point to be stressed here is that for Plato Being is not simply the possibility of predication, it is an actual attribute of things (cf. Marten, 207)—in terms of the theory of Forms, it is an all-pervasive Kind (γένος), clearly well up the ontological hierarchy, possessing a nature of its own, and regarded by Plato as the cause of the being of all other things (just as the Other, which turns out to be Not-being, is a real entity and the cause of the differences that exist in the world, as is stated at 255e). I think the note in which Owen (233, n. 20) attempts to read the distinction between predicates and abstract entities into the *Sophist* shows that the disease of anachronism has at least a foothold in his approach. This is not in any sense to reject the approach through logic, but simply to ensure that it is balanced and filled out by the sort of exploration of the metaphysical implications which Bluck supplies.

Within a very thorough and illuminating discussion, which goes much further than Bluck in, for example, analysing the precise stages of the statement of the 'puzzles' about Being and Not-being, there are a couple of unresolved difficulties. The first concerns a methodological principle basic to Owen's interpretation which he calls the 'Parity Assumption' (230). This is drawn from a very strict reading of 250e, the passage where the hope is expressed that, 'what is' and 'what is not' being equally puzzling, any light thrown on one will be equally revealing for the other. Owen takes this to exclude *a priori* all interpretations of the dialogue which allow any meaning to positive uses of the verb 'to be' which they disallow for negative occurrences. But 250e is the dramatic fulcrum of the dialogue, marking the change from an aporetic to an illuminatory mood. Can we really be justified in reading so much more into it than it actually states?

The second problem is this. Rightly stressing the distinction Plato draws between negation and opposition (257b f., 258e), Owen finds the predicative function of 'is' and 'is not' adequate to explain all the usages of the verb which Plato discusses in the dialogue. A positive assertion that x is will always be incomplete and elliptical for 'x is y'; a negative assertion that x is not will also require completion—'x is not z'. 'Plato, or his speakers in the dialogue', writes Owen (234), 'can find no intelligible contrary to being or to what is (258e6–259a1). But, he insists, this breeds no confusion in the notion of speaking of what is not.' The reason for this is that the contrary of '. . . is . . .' could only be, Owen claims (235), 'a subject which for every predicate F is not F'.

The fallacy which vitiates Owen's view, however, is that he has established precisely what he and Plato claim to have avoided, namely a relationship of opposition between Being and Not-being. On his view 'is' implies 'is y': Being, to use the abstract noun, may therefore be defined as 'possession of some property'. 'Is not' always implies 'is not y': Not-being is therefore the non-possession of a property. Now, while the properties Y and not-Y are, as Plato claims, not necessarily opposites, possession and non-possession of Y are: there is no middle state such as Owen postulates. And he is very insistent (236 ff.) that Plato is not simply reducing 'without remainder' 'is-not y' to 'is not-y'. 'Is not' (and the Form to which the expression refers, Not-being) has an independent nature of its own as a real, though incomplete, predicate.

Owen claims, with some plausibility, that the opposite (for which he uses the term 'contrary' throughout) of Being (defined as possessing some attribute) would be to possess no attributes at all, and that this fits perfectly with Plato's statement that there can be no subject for any proposition with that predicate: 'is not' is in fact 'applicable only to subjects in the middle state' (235)—on Owen's view to subjects which possess some but do not possess other attributes. But put his thesis the other way round and the mistake becomes obvious. The opposite of Not-being in this sense, i.e. in the sense of possessing *no* attributes, would be Being in the sense of possessing not some but *all* attributes. Surely a Being to outdo Parmenides, even!

Plato should probably not be pressed into a strict logical straitjacket as far as concerns his use of the distinction between an opposite and what negation means. He certainly has in mind alongside an uncompromising sense of Not-being, opposed to Being in a strongly polarized relationship and such that it is not applicable to any subject, a more innocuous type which is related less implacably to Being: Owen is surely right (236) to understand Plato as concerned here with the fact that 'a subject must be identified and characterized as well as differentiated'. But the fact that it seems impossible to accommodate the polarized opposite and the more innocuous negation of Being on the same continuum is strong evidence against the thesis that we are dealing throughout the *Sophist* with a purely copulative role for the verb 'to be'.

3. THE 'SOPHIST' AS A TREATISE ON NEGATION

In hazarding yet another interpretation of what must often seem an insoluble problem, I would want to lay stress on certain facts about the *Sophist* which seem to me not to have been given due attention. They make me doubt that the dialogue is an analysis of the verb 'to be' at all. I mean this in two senses: (i) it is not Plato's main purpose to clear up the ambiguity of 'is' (ἔστιν) in Greek; (ii) he does not in fact offer any distinction between senses of the verb. There is linguistic analysis, but it centres, I believe, around the negative, not the verb 'to be', and even then it is analysis employed as a means to an end rather than 'pure' analysis.

The facts I base this conclusion on are these. First, no examples are discussed of positive statements of identity, but only negative statements of non-identity. True, the series of Divisions contain, in Cornford's sense (296), uses of identitative 'is', but the central exposition does not appear to relate to the method of Division as such. What we are offered is much more a comparison of pairs of positive and negative statements, apparent contradictions of the form '*x* is *y*', '*x* is not *y*'.

Second, towards the end of the section on the five Kinds, the problem of 'what is not' is explicitly subsumed under the general problem of negation (257bc). It is a difficult, tantalizingly compressed argument; and the incomplete nature of Bluck's discussion of it is equally tantalizing. In any case Plato is probably, to an extent at least, misguided if his aim is, as appears, to prove that 'what is not' (τὸ μὴ ὄν) is no less real than 'what is' (τὸ ὄν). Granted that 'not large' does not necessarily imply its opposite 'small', it does, as used

here, imply 'less large than large'. The distinction between contrariety and opposition is not therefore fully
appropriate to Plato's purposes so long as he continues,
as he still seems to at 258e8 f., to regard the 'totally unreal'
(or some such) as a candidate for the role of opposite.
But these detailed criticisms apart, it is surely clear that
Plato sees the problem in terms of the analysis of what
in general the negative (μή or οὔ) signifies.

Third, although Plato offers an analysis of non-
identity 'is not' statements, his method is to reduce the
'not' rather than the 'is' to other terms. Thus at 255e ff.
'Change is not (e.g.) the Same', is derived from 'Change
is different from the Same'. Significantly, this analysis
does not apply to positive statements of identity, which
would have to be derived from a different source, viz.
'the same as'. It is therefore completely misleading to
claim that Plato has distinguished the 'is' of identity as
such. And if we ask why he did not simply analyse 'is not'
into 'is not the same as', the answer must surely be the
obvious one: it would have made no direct contribution
to the aim of vindicating the ontological status of 'what
is not'. In other words, the negative is his main worry.

Fourth, Plato's use of 'the Same', which has been
claimed, for example by Ackrill, to be the periphrasis for
positive statements of identity, shows some rather serious
idiosyncrasies. Plato never uses it, as we would have
expected him to, to explain what are in fact the normal
occurrences of identitative 'is', those in propositions of
the '*a* is *b*' type where *a*=*b*, e.g. 'The London–Holyhead
road is the A 5.' Instead it always refers to the 'self-
identity' of a single thing, e.g. Change at 256a, not to the
relationship between two terms (or descriptions) referring
to the same entity. A possible exception is the argument

at 255bc for the separateness of Being and the Same, but this is a casual reference and suspect for other reasons (see Bluck's discussion). It is not offered as any sort of analysis of 'is'. Crombie is more guarded than Ackrill, but still proceeds rather to beg the question when he writes (vol. II, p. 407): 'He would no doubt be willing to use "A partakes in sameness to B" to identify A and B.' Cf. also Owen (251). The fact remains that such cases are avoided.

Fifth, in the second of the four contrasting pairs of attributes predicated of Change (255e ff.), Plato specifically refers to the ambiguity (οὐ . . . ὁμοίως εἰρήκαμεν) which is involved in calling Change both the Same and not the Same. But since he explains the ambiguity as centring round the words 'the Same' and 'not the Same', we would be somewhat obstinate to see here any evidence that he is concerned with the ambiguity of the verb 'to be'. See also Kamlah (41) and Frede (11) on this passage. Once again it is the word 'not' in the phrase 'not the Same' which is analysed—as 'other than'. To Plato what is involved is not so much an ambiguity of language as a paradox of ontological fact. It arises quite simply because Change, like all other Forms, partakes at once of Sameness and Difference (Otherness).

The conclusion I draw from these facts has emerged already. To place the main emphasis of analysis on the negative does not rob the *Sophist* of its status as an answer to Parmenides, and is perhaps in keeping with modern interpretations of that philosopher in which the ambiguity of 'is' is in any case of less importance. Certainly to hunt down the Sophist, it is a perfectly valid approach, if successful, to show that the negative may be shorthand for a thoroughly positive predicate, namely 'different from'. And that appears to me to be what Plato has signposted throughout the dialogue as his aim.

How successful is he? To a degree, in my opinion, but not entirely. Not that it is easy to judge his success in terms of the explicit aims of the dialogue, because he does not explain how the analysis of negation applies to the existence of images. We are left to draw our own conclusions from the not very explicit application to false statements at 263b, helped, perhaps, by faint echoes detectable between that passage and 240b. (Perhaps this deficiency is evidence that Plato was interested in vindicating negation as much for its own sake as for the specific applications suggested by the dramatic context of the dialogue.)

The discussion of non-identity between Kinds as far as 257a is apt enough as a demonstration that non-identity is a thoroughly positive property, namely Difference (Otherness). The examples given are drawn from a limited range of special cases, i.e. non-identity between Forms where one is an attribute of the other: for example, Change partakes of Being but is not identical with it. In such cases, the non-identity is explained as the reverse side of the coin to something basic and fundamental to each Form, its own absolute self-identity. For Change, non-identity with (Difference from) all other Forms is a necessary condition of its being Change. Plato may therefore claim to have established the fact that Difference is a very positive and highly significant property.

Although Plato has been concerned with special cases, there are no real difficulties about transferring the analysis to all cases of non-identity. The restriction to cases where one term is an attribute of the other is probably dramatically motivated: it allows for a pointedly paradoxical style

(x is and is not y), and it closely parallels the case of images, where it is precisely the image of (e.g.) Socrates of which we would be most likely to assert that it is not Socrates. But the analysis holds for other cases of non-identity too. The only question might arise in connexion with non-identity between particular instances of the same Form: where x and y are both (e.g.) dogs, is their mutual non-identity similarly related to their essential self-identity? The answer is probably that for a Platonist it isn't, but he would not be concerned to assert the non-identity, or even the individual self-identity, of objects of Becoming as an article of truth anyway, while a non-Platonist would be quite willing to accept the self-identity of the individual as basic.

When Plato extends his analysis to negative predication, problems arise. Some concern such detailed points as the relevance of the contrary–opposite distinction (see above). On the question whether Plato was himself aware of the difference between negative identity and negative predication there is also disagreement. While I accept that from 257b we are concerned with what is in fact negative predication, I do not share Bluck's view that Plato had the distinction clear in his own mind. Bluck's view is not proved by the fact that Plato devotes a separate section to the problem, because other explanations are possible for this. The most probable will be in terms of the Form-particular dichotomy. Plato will quite plausibly, I suggest, have thought it necessary to demonstrate independently that the same analysis could be applied to negative statements involving both Forms and particulars as to those dealing with Forms alone.

In practice, the analysis is effective. There are defects, but they are not fatal if the aim is to interpret negative statements as positive in content. Wiggins makes a similar point about falsehood: he writes (302), 'Plato's objective was as much to *find room* for falsity as to define it . . .; and in the former project I believe he has more success.' When we deny an attribute, it is usually to make a definite point, e.g. to correct or prevent a mistake. And the 'mistake', actual or likely, may well be regarded as a misattribution of a property (to the Platonist, a Form) to the subject in question. I am likely to state 'Deirdre is not beautiful' when I not only think the opposite view may be held, but also have myself made a positive assessment of the girl and find her aesthetic properties essentially different from Beauty—as a consequence, be it noted, of the specific self-identity of both Beauty itself and (e.g.) Obesity itself! Difference from Beauty, as Plato says, is no less a reality than Beauty itself.

But what is practically effective may be inadequate at the level of philosophical analysis. And there is a serious flaw in the exposition if it is judged as a theory of negative predication. However, the danger of confusing our conceptual framework with Plato's makes it very difficult to assess whether the flaw is fatal in its own context or not.

As an analysis of negative predication, we may say that *either* it does not work *or* it involves an important shift in the meaning of 'the Other' (θάτερον). In the previous section the statement (e.g.) that 'Change partakes of Difference (Otherness) from Being' asserted the non-identity of Change and Being but did not exclude the attribution of Being to Change (except perhaps in respect of the essential nature of Change). So if we are to interpret the present analysis in the same way, 'the Not-beautiful' will be simply Difference from Beauty. But (e.g.) Shapeliness, though a species of Beauty, is also different from Beauty in this sense. On the present view, therefore, Shapeliness will be included in what can be described as 'not beautiful'. So will Helen herself—which might not worry Plato with his doctrine of Becoming, but will remain a problem for many of his readers!

Hence the suggestion that 'the Different (the Other)' here means 'incompatible'. Bluck rejects this interpretation (for references see p. 163, n. 2)—rightly, I believe—on the grounds that if Plato had wanted to express the idea of incompatibility he could have done so easily and without ambiguity. The point can be made more positive. At 263b7 he does express what amounts to incompatibility in the phrase 'other than the things that are [about you]' (ἕτερα τῶν ὄντων). And he achieves this without any equivocation over the sense of 'other'.

But even if we grant the rendering 'incompatible', it does not rescue Plato. It is true that, plagued by obesity, both Deirdre and her aesthetic properties (Obesity, Ugliness, etc.) would be incompatible with Beauty. But the problem then is how to reconcile this passage with the earlier discussion. Incompatibility is totally unsuitable as an explanation of non-identity. Can Plato be guilty of confusion or ambiguity of this order? I am unwilling to believe so, especially since his paradoxical form of expression earlier deliberately focused our attention on the special cases of non-identity between Forms which do in fact mix (e.g. Change and Being). If he was now consciously presenting a formula intended to exclude precisely those cases, it would be unthinkable that he should confuse us by using so similar a form of words.

But what does our flaw amount to if we are right that Plato was not concerned formally either to analyse negation or to distinguish identity and predication? It largely boils away. He has provided a positive content for sentences of the type 'x is not y' both where x is not identical with y and where x does not have the attribute Y. And he has done this in such a way as to vindicate the apparently meaningless concept of Not-being. Statements of both types assert a definite attribute, namely Difference (Otherness) or more precisely the 'part of the Other that is set in contrast to' y. Not-being or 'what is not' is precisely this, Difference or 'what is other'.

The defect we have been discussing, that this analysis seems to allow for statements of the type 'Helen is not beautiful', statements which are by definition false, exists only if we insist on treating negative predication as a separate thing. Plato's own answer could well be to assimilate statements of this type to that of 'Change is not Being', and to argue that 'Helen is different from Beauty' gives a positive and true meaning to the statement in question: we must not fault him for not answering twentieth-century problems. (Although this is a different interpretation from Bluck's, it is considerably helped by his emphasis on the paradeigmatic role of the Forms: see p. 160, n. 2.)

I would not deny, of course, that negation covers a much wider range of statement than Plato considers. He certainly makes no attempt to apply his analysis to (e.g.) 'Not all girls are beautiful' or 'It is not the case that p'. In this respect, his vindication of negation fails by sheer default. So much so, that this is, I suspect, one major reason why so many commentators have failed to recognize the *Sophist* as a discussion of negation at all, and have preferred to see it as a solution to the problems of the verb 'to be'.

CHAPTER I: 216a–231b
IN SEARCH OF THE SOPHIST

I. THE CHARACTERS AND THE OPENING CONVERSATION

At the opening of the dialogue Theodorus greets Socrates with the remark that he and Theaetetus have returned 'faithful to our appointment of yesterday'. This connects the *Sophist* with the dialogue *Theaetetus*; and the *Statesman* is in turn connected by its opening remarks with the *Sophist*. Probably it is implied that there is at least some connexion in doctrine between the three works, and certainly the *Statesman* investigates the nature of the Statesman in the same sort of way that the *Sophist* investigates the nature of the Sophist. But any opinion about the connexion between these three works must depend very largely on one's interpretation of the *Theaetetus* and *Sophist*, and a pronouncement upon it must be left over for the moment.[1]

At the same time Theodorus introduces to Socrates an Eleatic visitor (henceforward referred to as 'the EV'), whom he describes as 'truly philosophic'. When Socrates ironically suggests that he must be a sort of 'god of refutation', Theodorus insists that he is in fact more reasonable than those who devote themselves to eristic; Socrates remarks that those who are 'not feignedly but really philosophers' are difficult to recognize, and on account of the ignorance of the general public are often

---

[1] [If, as this paragraph suggests, Bluck was planning to conclude the book with a survey of the *Sophist*'s place in Plato's later writings, no trace or outline of this is to be found among his papers.]

mistaken for statesmen, sophists, and sometimes even madmen. All this, combined with Socrates' expression of gratitude to Theodorus at the beginning of the *States-man* for having introduced him to the EV, clearly means that we are to take seriously what the EV has to say.

It remains possible, of course, to take much of what he says as verbal quibbling designed to defeat the eristics at their own game, and his purpose to be that of revealing some of the linguistic fallacies of the eristics. Eristic argument seems to have been practised by, among others, the followers of Euclides at Megara (cf. Diogenes Laertius II.106–7), who in some ways continued the Eleatic tradition. But it is not obvious why Plato should choose an Eleatic as a *dramatis persona* through whom to criticize Eleatic eristic. The insistence, moreover, that the EV is not a specialist in refutation makes it rather un-likely that he is about to attack the eristics with their own weapons. The description of him as a 'true philosopher' leads us rather to expect that his remarks will have a more direct and important bearing on Plato's own philosophy.

However one interprets the *Parmenides*, Parmenides' own remarks in that dialogue had clearly had such a bearing, and we may reasonably look for a similar con-tribution, though perhaps of a more constructive nature, from the EV now. Plato had followed Parmenides in distinguishing between what is intelligible and what is perceptible, but at the same time his theory encountered the same difficulty as did the Parmenidean 'one', that serious consequences arise if 'nothing has any capacity for combination with anything else for any purpose' (251e–252a). If he regarded himself before as the heir of Parmenides, he might now represent his theory, amended

so as to allow for Communion of Forms, as a further
development along the same line of thought, the product
of an enlightened Eleaticism.

The EV is an enlightened or reformed Eleatic, just as
the materialists whose views are discussed at 246–7 are
reformed materialists. Plato thought it unlikely that
materialists could ever in reality be reformed in the way
here imagined (246d, 247c), and he would probably have
admitted that the EV as a character is not very plausible
either. But the enlightenment in each case is assumed for
the sake of the argument; and a truly enlightened Eleaticism would correspond, in Plato's view, to Platonism.

Socrates asks whether the EV's countrymen regarded
Sophist, Statesman and Philosopher as three distinct
types of person (216d–217a). The EV replies that they did,
but that these types are difficult to define. Socrates urges
him nevertheless to make an attempt at definition, and
asks whether he prefers the method of continuous exposition or the method of asking questions—the latter
being the method which 'Parmenides used once in my
presence to expound some excellent arguments, when I
was young and he was very old' (217c).

There is here a clear allusion to the dialogue *Parmenides*.
Cornford infers (169) that it 'emphasizes the contrast
between Eleatic methods of argument and the genuine
dialectic of Socrates and Plato, already illustrated by the
Theaetetus'. But it is difficult to understand the present
allusion to the *Parmenides* in any such sense. Cornford
seems to have in mind a contrast between the *Parmenides*,
which he describes as an 'exhibition of Zenonian dialectic', and the *Sophist*, which he apparently regards as an
example, like the *Theaetetus*, of 'the genuine dialectic'.[1]

---

[1] Cornford (169) acknowledges that in the *Sophist* 'the description of

But there is no distinction of method between these dialogues. The method which the EV chooses, that of asking questions, is the method linked with Parmenides here and in fact used in the dialogue named after him.

Nor is it plausible to suppose that the methods of *both* the *Parmenides* and the *Sophist* are being contrasted with genuine dialectic, since the latter was itself conducted 'by means of questions', and the EV's method is basically similar to the Socratic in that it is one of co-operative enquiry (218b). The EV's utterances certainly tend to be lengthy. But he apologizes for this in advance (217d–e), and it is accounted for by the difficulty of the task he has undertaken. Otherwise, as Cornford says (170), 'once the conversation is started, his manner is distinguished by no individual trait from that of the Platonic Socrates'.

It may be doubted whether the allusion to the *Parmenides* has any important significance of this kind. We are simply being reminded of an earlier critique of Platos' theory of Forms from an 'enlightened Eleatic' point of view, a critique which revealed weaknesses (whether real or only apparent) that have now to be corrected.

Encouraged to attempt the task of definition, the EV accepts Theaetetus as his respondent and begins by considering the Sophist. As the Sophist is hard to define, he proposes to consider and define first a lesser thing, which may be used as a pattern (παράδειγμα) for the greater (218d). The lesser thing chosen is Angling, and the definition of this is followed by several different attempts to define the Sophist.

the Stranger makes clear that he does not stand for this negative and destructive element [viz. eristic] in the Eleatic tradition. The reader is not to expect an exhibition of Zenonian dialectic, such as we had in the *Parmenides*.'

2. THE METHOD OF DIVISION

The definitions reached define by genus and specific differences. They are set out in diagram form in an appendix to this chapter. The method adopted is that of Collection and Division, described in the *Phaedrus* (265d–265e). The procedure has been succinctly described by Taylor (*Plato*, 377):

If we wish to define a species *x*, we begin by taking some wider and familiar class *a* of which *x* is clearly one subdivision. We then devise a division of the whole class *a* into two mutually exclusive sub-classes *b* and *c*, distinguished by the fact that *b* possesses, while *c* lacks, some characteristic β which we know to be found in *x*. We call *b* the right-hand, *c* the left-hand, division of *a*. We now leave the left-hand division *c* out of consideration, and proceed to subdivide the right-hand division *b* on the same principle as before, and this process is repeated until we come to a right-hand 'division' which we see on inspection to coincide with *x*. If we now assign the original wider class *a* and enumerate in order the successive characters by which each of the successive right-hand divisions has been marked off, we have a complete characterization of *x*; *x* has been defined.

In 'devising a division' of a class or sub-class the EV apparently considers the members of it and collects them together into groups.[1] Probably, in fact, a Collection is made before each Division, though sometimes the collect-

---

[1] The method is not explained precisely. Hackforth (*Plato's Examination of Pleasure*, 143) notes that 'at 220c, where Fishing is divided into fishing by enclosure and fishing by striking, the former kind is reached by a Collection of varieties of enclosure'. Sometimes only one group is isolated: at 267a–b the EV says, 'Let us reserve that section, then, under the name of mimicry, and indulge ourselves so far as to leave all the rest for someone else to collect into a unity and give it an appropriate name.'

ing process receives no open mention. The 'parts' into which each class is ultimately divided should represent specific Forms (*Statesman* 262b, cf. *Phaedrus* 265e); divisions should be made only where there is a real cleavage, and this means considering real *things*, not merely *names*.[1] All this will apply whether the method is used for an attempt at a complete classification of all the species falling under a genus, or, as Plato commonly uses it, for the definition of a single species. Where the only aim is definition, a complete classification is not necessary, or at any rate not normally attempted in the Divisions found in the *Sophist* and *Statesman*. Thus in the *Sophist* all arts are divided into productive and acquisitive, while in the *Statesman* they are divided into theoretical and practical; and Cornford (172) points out that in the series of Divisions whereby the EV reaches his definition of Angling, 'the shift of principle from prey to method would vitiate the scheme as a classification of hunting: land animals and birds may equally well be netted or struck'.

Mere use of the formal method of Collection and Division is no guarantee of the correctness of a resulting definition. Aristotle (*An. Pr.* 46a31 ff.) seems to have thought that the method was regarded as capable of *proving* what the nature of a thing was, but no doubt 'Plato would have agreed with the statement that a definition of essence cannot be demonstrated in the logical sense of demonstration' (Skemp, 70; cf. Taylor, *Plato*, 377–8, Gulley, 111 f.). The interrelated structure of the world of Forms is certainly supposed to correspond closely to the structure of the phenomenal world, and

[1] Cf. 218c. Often a genuine Form may have no particular name in common use: cf. 267a–b, and *Statesman* 260e, 261e.

the dialectician can use the evidence of this world in devising his Collections and Divisions. But even this means that the formal method must be supplemented by the dialectician's experience.

The dialectician has to choose a genus from which to start: in both the *Sophist* and the *Statesman* the genus originally chosen is abandoned and a new start is made with a new one. He has to choose each new right-hand division, and know when his *definiendum* has been sufficiently specified. Likewise the definitions reached may not correctly represent the relationship of the *definienda* to the other Forms that are mentioned; and they may also be incorrect in what they allege about the nature and interrelationship of these other Forms.

All this presupposes a certain prior knowledge of the nature of that object, as well as of the nature of the genus that he chooses. Furthermore a complete classification would normally be so vast that he must depend upon some sort of insight to guide him in the course of his dividing. It is difficult to avoid the conclusion that this insight is what Plato would have called Recollection of the Forms concerned.[1]

That the method depends upon a certain amount of pre-existing knowledge becomes even more obvious when one considers the use made of 'examples' (παραδεί-γματα). At 218d, indeed, it appears that the purpose of defining Angling is simply to acquire experience in the method of Division by practising it on something com-

---

[1] So far as Collection is concerned, this is explicitly stated at *Phaedrus* 249b–c, but as this occurs in the speech which Socrates later (265b–c) refers to as 'mythical', it is unsafe to rely on this passage alone. Had Plato ever abandoned his theory of Recollection, we might have expected Aristotle to say so. For a fuller discussion see Gulley, 108 ff., and, on the relationship between definition and Recollection, Bluck, *Logos and Forms,* a reply to Cross, *Logos and Forms.*

paratively easy before trying to define the Sophist; but
at 221d the EV asks, 'Have we failed to recognize that
the one man (the Angler) is akin to the other (the Sophist)?' They both seem to him to be hunters, and he
proceeds to define the Sophist by starting, 'with no
explicit justification' as Cornford (173) says, from the
genus Hunting. It looks as though there was a special
reason other than its easiness to define for the choice of
Angling as an 'example'.[1]

This is confirmed by the evidence of the *Statesman*,
where the EV, whose aim has been to define the Statesman, looks for an example which must be something
trivial (σμικρότατον) but something which 'involves the
same sort of activity as Statesmanship' and 'would enable
us to discover satisfactorily what we seek' (279a–b). The
discussion of the example chosen, the art of Weaving,
serves indeed to show the necessity of separating off
kindred and subservient arts; but we also find, in the
subsequent discussion of Statesmanship, that an *analogy*
is assumed to exist between Weaving and Statesmanship
(305e–6a): the statesman has to weave together in the
state the courageous and the moderate—the warp, as it
were, and the weft. Indeed, we are given a preliminary
account at 277d ff. of how an 'example' (παράδειγμα)
should function. Elements with which we are familiar in
one setting we may fail to recognize in another, but a
comparison may help us to recognize them in both
(277e–278d); and thus the EV proposes, in taking a lesser
thing as an example, to reveal the character (εἶδος) which
Statesmanship shares with it (278e). Now, the ability
to choose a suitable 'example' presupposes an existing
consciousness that there is a certain analogy with the

[1] Cf. appendix to this chapter.

thing chosen, and this would seem to be best explained as a partial Recollection of the Forms.[1]

It is doubtful whether Plato would have regarded even a correct definition by genus and species as capable of conveying knowledge. Cornford (170) reminds us of the *Theaetetus*, where in a discussion ostensibly at least confined to individual concrete things it is concluded that the addition of a *logos* of such a thing to a true notion of it could not yield knowledge, and remarks, ' "The Sophist" is not an individual, but a species; and the addition of a *logos* in a new sense—a definition by genus and specific differences—can lead to knowledge of the nature of a species.' But the mere introduction of this kind of *logos*, not mentioned in the *Theaetetus*, need not mean that Plato has abandoned his conception of a Form as an individual thing, to be known only by a sort of acquaintance (γνῶσις). Certainly he now regards Forms as interrelated, and these relationships can be described; one can, as it were, plot the position of a Form on a map (Skemp, 74); but it does not follow that Plato would have regarded the statement of certain relationships as a statement of the essence (οὐσία) of a Form. Furthermore, a definition of this kind could not convey knowledge unless all the Forms corresponding to the terms employed were 'known'; and the same will apply to definitions of each of these Forms, and so on.

---

[1] [It is difficult to be sure how far the use of 'examples' in the *Sophist* and *Statesman* is one of Plato's literary or educational techniques rather than, as Bluck implies, an exercise capable of aiding the individual's own groping towards a definition. The EV is presented in the role not of the researcher but of the expert choosing the best tool for the instruction of his pupil. And the neatness of the analogies is obviously due to Plato's own skill in composing dialogues. All this, however, is simply to strengthen Bluck's claim that Collection and Division depend upon pre-existing knowledge.]

Again, in the *Theaetetus* it was agreed that the ability correctly to enumerate the parts of a thing cannot be said to convert a correct notion of that thing into knowledge of it, since it may happen that one is unable correctly to enumerate those same parts in a different situation (206e–208b). The example given is of someone who might correctly write THE as the first syllable of the name Theaetetus, but misspell the same syllable in writing the name Theodorus: he cannot be said to know that syllable. Now in the *Statesman* (277d–278e) we are told that it is precisely because elements with which we are familiar in one setting (and of which we have a 'correct opinion') we may fail to recognize in another—like children who recognize letters in one syllable but fail to recognize those same letters in another—that it is useful for the dialectician to make use of 'examples' (παραδείγματα). This suggests that the layman who is able to define (say) Weaving satisfactorily but not Statesmanship could not be said to have knowledge of what Weaving and Statesmanship have in common, and that therefore his definition of Weaving, which includes those common elements, though quite correct so far as it goes, does not constitute and could not convey knowledge of the essence of Weaving. It would merely reflect a true opinion.

The whole procedure appears to be one not of discovery but of clarification—a systematic attempt to actualize pre-existing latent knowledge. As Cherniss has said, 'diairesis appears to be only an aid to reminiscence of the idea': it is 'merely a practical expedient for recalling the essential nature of a given object' (vol. 1, 47; 60, n. 50). The method of Division is at least foreshadowed in the *Gorgias* (463e ff.; see Dodds *ad loc.*),

but it is not there associated with the search for knowledge, and in the *Meno*, *Phaedo* and *Republic*, where the
search for knowledge is discussed, it finds no place. It
would seem therefore that definition by Collection and
Division comes to the fore as a technique for improving
one's Recollection of the Forms from the time of the
Phaedrus onwards. If this is so, it may be regarded as a
system devised in accordance with the implication of the
Meno that the best way to achieve knowledge is by continued attempts at definition, which will prompt Recollection (see further Bluck, *Meno* 16 f., 43 f., 58 f.).
The conduct of the method will be dependent upon at
least partial Recollection, and its aim will be further
Recollection.

The question now arises, why are we presented with
several different series of Divisions, each of which reaches
a different definition of the Sophist? This question is
closely bound up with the question who the practitioners
of the cathartic method, defined in series 6, are supposed
to be.

3. THE 'SOPHISTRY OF NOBLE FAMILY'

(a) *The identity of the practitioners.* Series 6 (226b ff.) starts
from a genus neither mentioned nor suggested in any of
the earlier series, and describes what has usually been
taken as the activity of Socrates himself.[1] It is indisput-
able that here 'satire is dropped' and that 'the tone is
serious and sympathetic'; and commentators have found
its inclusion puzzling. An attempt by Professor Kerferd
(84) to interpret it as referring to sophists has been

[1] Cf. Cornford, 177. Taylor (*Plato,* 381), however, sees here 'inferior
imitators of the dialectic', Robinson (11 ff.) an allusion to methods
employed in Plato's earlier dialogues.

rejected by other writers (Booth, 89; Trevaskis, 36). While some of their criticisms of particular arguments are cogent, a point has been overlooked which, as we shall see, strongly favours Kerferd's main contention.

The practitioners of the art with which we are here concerned are engaged in purifying the soul. Of the two evils of the soul (227d), one is a 'disease' (νόσος) resulting from 'discord' (στάσις) and taken to account for what men call 'wickedness' (πονηρία). This has to be treated by punishment. The other is an 'ugliness' (αἶσχος)[1] due to a lack of proportion (ἀμετρία), which results in 'ignorance' (ἄγνοια); and of ignorance there is more than one kind. Thinking that one knows a thing when one does not know it is called 'stupidity' (ἀμαθία), and whereas other kinds are to be remedied by technical instruction, this kind calls for 'education' (παιδεία) by means of a process of cross-questioning (ἔλεγχος) which shows the patient's opinions to be mutually contradictory and thereby removes his conceit of wisdom. This is the activity which is attributed, albeit with a certain amount of irony, to the Sophist, in a passage (230e–231b) that has given rise to a good deal of controversy:

EV. Well, who shall we say the practitioners of this art are? I hesitate to say 'sophists'.

Theaet. Why?

EV. For fear of according them too high an honour.

Theaet. And yet the present description resembles such a person.

EV. So does a wolf resemble a dog, a very fierce animal a very tame one. But the cautious man must always be on his

[1] This word is usually translated 'deformity', but its primary meaning is simply 'ugliness'. It will be suggested presently that Plato may have in mind not a lack of proportion within the soul (such as 'deformity' might suggest) but a lack of proportion between soul and body. See p. 48f.

guard in the matter of resemblances, more than in anything else, for they are a most slippery kind of thing. However, let them be sophists; for I think that when people are
sufficiently on their guard[1] their disputes will be about
distinctions of no small importance.

Theaet. Probably so.

EV. Let us take it, then, that part of the separating art is
purification, and that the kind of purification which has to
do with the soul has been distinguished, and as a species
of this, instruction, and as a species of instruction, education; and as a species of education, let the cross-questioning of the vain conceit of wisdom, just mentioned in the
discussion, be said to be nothing other than the sophistry
of noble family.

Some of the points at issue here are not very important.
Probably it is to the sophists rather than to the practitioners of cross-questioning that the EV is afraid of
according too high an honour (231a3) (so Kerferd, 85
and Trevaskis, 37, against Cornford, 180, n. 2). Probably,
too, no direct equation is intended between the practitioner and the dog on the one hand, or between the
sophist and the wolf on the other (so Kerferd, 85 and
Trevaskis, 37 f.); and if this is so, while it is no doubt
true that the point about the dog and the wolf must be
that 'their superficial resemblance disguises their real
natures which are poles apart' (Trevaskis, 38), we need
not suppose that the practitioner and the sophist are
thought of as being *as* different from each other as the
dog is from the wolf. The overt meaning will simply be

---

[1] On the meaning of the verb here, Kerferd (86) is probably right, in
view of its undoubted meaning immediately above. (Cornford translates
the sentence, 'should they ever set up an adequate defence of their confines, the boundary in dispute will be of no small importance', and Taylor
takes it in much the same way.) If φυλάττωσι is the correct reading, the
subject may be understood as 'people' in general.

that appearances can be deceptive, and that there *may* be an important difference. But there is certainly a strong implication both that in this general area there *are* distinctions to be drawn, and (if the negative at 231a9–b1 is taken, as is most natural, with σμικρῶν) that they are in fact distinctions 'of no small importance' (Trevaskis, 38–9, Booth, 89).

Yet if the description has really been a description of Socrates' method only, and the distinctions between him and the sophists are such that they are 'poles apart', it is exceedingly difficult to understand why Theaetetus regards the account of Socrates' method as resembling that of the Sophist (231a). It is also difficult to understand why an account of Socrates' method should have been included at all, for at 232a the EV seems to suggest that there is some single element common to all the skills with which the Sophist has been credited in all the preceding series of Divisions, and at 232b ff. he proceeds to look for it.

Here a point that has not hitherto been noticed may be of some assistance. It has been maintained by the EV that as, in the case of the body, medicine deals with disease and gymnastics with ugliness, so 'the corrective art, of all arts the one most closely related to Justice', deals with disease of the soul, and instruction with ugliness of soul (228e–229a); and it is with ugliness of soul that the practitioners of the cathartic art described are concerned. Now the *Gorgias* similarly compares the arts that deal with the body and those that deal with the soul, treating legislation and justice as corresponding to gymnastics and medicine respectively. The choice of the former pair, which have to do with society as a whole, is no doubt determined by the desire to explain rhetoric as the counterfeit of a branch of politics (463d; so Dodds *ad loc.*): if he had had the individual soul in mind, Plato might have substituted instruction for legislation. But the important point is that each of the four arts is said to have its spurious imitation, which is not an art at all but purely empirical in character and aiming not at what is best but simply at what is pleasing. These four spurious imitations, each of which is a form of flattery, are the following: cookery, imitating medicine; beauty culture, imitating gymnastics; rhetoric, imitating justice; and sophistry, imitating legislation. It looks as though, at the time of the *Gorgias* anyhow, Plato regarded sophistry as a *spurious imitation* of the art which, in the case of the soul, corresponds to gymnastics in the case of the body.

If he still regards it in this way, he must regard it as a spurious imitation of the true art of curing ugliness of soul; and that he does so is borne out by 268b–c, where the Sophist in the final series of Divisions is said to be an ignorant imitator of the philosopher. Probably we should conclude that the final series of Divisions is meant to reveal the element common to all the skills attributed to the Sophist in *all* the earlier series, including the sixth,[1] and that the 'skill' represented in this sixth series is something in which the Sophist does resemble Socrates (or the true philosopher), though only to the extent to which a counterfeit imitation resembles a genuine article. This view will allow us to treat the sixth description as at any rate giving some indication of an aspect of sophistry or of a kind of sophist, and to understand Theaetetus' remark that it 'resembles' a sophist.

If we ask why we are given what could be taken as a description of Socrates' method, the answer may be that

---

[1] [Cf. Cornford, 187; but see Sayre, 154 f.]

a good way of describing a counterfeit method is to indicate the genuine method that it imitates. While we are not explicitly told here that we have to do with an imitation, we are given a warning that if we are on our guard we may detect an important difference between the (genuine) practitioner of the cathartic art and the sophist, and the nature of this difference is made plain in the final series of Divisions (268b–c). The Sophist is a bogus practitioner, and his motives and achievements are not the high ones attributed to him at 230b–d. But so far as what he professes and his procedure are concerned, it is hard to find anything in the description here that is obviously inapplicable, and there is a good deal that is quite true.

Admittedly, all ignorance is said to be involuntary (228c7–8), but, as Kerferd (87) remarks, it is doubtful whether what is said here 'has even a limited reference to the Socratic doctrine that vice is due to ignorance'. The remark is made without reference to the *other* fault in the soul from which 'wickedness' arises, and even before the division of ignorance into 'stupidity' and mere lack of technical knowledge. Again, *all* ignorance is treated as needing to be remedied by instruction (229a), although we are told that popular opinion does not admit that ignorance is an evil when it is 'only in the soul' (228d)—which probably refers to cases where it does not result in any obvious perversity or inability.[1] But a sophist might well allow himself to differ from popular

---

[1] That is, if we take the phrase to mean 'so long as it gives rise to no outward manifestation'. Taylor seems to take it to mean 'in the soul' as opposed to 'in the body': 'it is only when the ignorance results in some failure to co-ordinate bodily movements as in the man who "can't learn" how to manage his hands or feet, that it is popularly allowed to be a deformity'.

opinion in this matter,[1] and indeed it would be in the
interests of his business that he should. Certainly sophists
did purport to give instruction, and they did go in for
cross-questioning (the use of the elenchus);[2] and men
like Euthydemus did try to show people (even when
they were right) that what they thought they knew could
be refuted. It is therefore legitimate that the procedure
described should, at this stage of the discussion and with
the warnings that are given, be labelled 'sophistry'. The
full title, 'the sophistry of noble family', may be taken
as indicating that this procedure, unlike other aspects or
kinds of sophistry, is related (as an imitation) to the
noble art of true philosophy.[3]

(b) *Wickedness and ignorance*. What is said about wickedness
and ignorance calls for some further comment, in relation
to Plato's moral doctrine and his doctrine of the soul;
for there can be little doubt that, although the whole of
the present doctrine is ironically attributed, at least by
implication, to the counterfeit practitioner of the method
described, it is at the same time presented as the doctrine
of the true philosopher.

[1] It may be noted that Plato is probably not simply 'using the popular
view of the matter' (Kerferd, 88) here. At 228d–e the EV does not say
that he accepts the popular view that ignorance is not an evil if it is 'only
in the soul'. A false conceit of wisdom might presumably be 'only in the
soul', and it is difficult to believe that the EV—or Plato, if this is Platonic
doctrine—would then consider this 'source of all the mistakes of the
mind' (229c) not an evil. It is clearly implied, at least, that ignorance may
sometimes be 'only in the soul', and it would appear that any foolish soul
must be 'ugly and out of proportion' and in need of instruction. This
suggests that ignorance is in any circumstances an evil. But we cannot be
certain of this: see below, p. 51f.

[2] In the seventh and final series of Divisions the Sophist is described in
terms reminiscent of 230b as 'forcing those who converse with him to
contradict themselves' (268b).

[3] For this reason 'of noble family' seems a better rendering of γένει
γενναία than 'of noble lineage' (as Cornford renders it).

In the first place, the main distinction, that between
wickedness and ignorance, is not, as might at first sight
appear to be the case, contrary to Socrates' belief that
all wrongdoing is due to ignorance. It does not mean
that in some cases of moral evil ignorance is not involved.
Hackforth (118–19) has cogently argued that Plato makes
this distinction in order to remedy a defect in the doctrine of *Republic* IV, where he had failed to allow for the
fact that the reason can err *per se*, and not always because
of excess of passion and desire. Plato now overcom-
pensates for this defect by drawing a distinction which
seems to imply, contrary to his real belief, that *no* moral
ignorance springs from excess of passion and desire.
Wickedness, which is due to such an excess and to a
resultant discord between the parts of the soul and
domination of the rational element by the irrational,
would still certainly involve ignorance, and this is recognized in at least one passage (*Timaeus* 86c–d; cf. *Laws*
863b–c) where a similar distinction is made. But there
are cases where ignorance arises simply through a defect
of reason, and the true philosopher at any rate would no
doubt consider that such a fault could only be remedied,
if at all, by instruction.

There is one other and rather more puzzling point.
The 'ugliness' of soul which is ignorance is attributed
(228a–c) to some sort of disproportion (ἀμετρία), and
it is not at all clear from our passage what is supposed to
be out of proportion to what, or whether, and if so how,
this disproportion is to be distinguished from the 'discord' (στάσις) between parts of the soul that results in
wickedness. Hackforth (120) concludes that it must be a
disproportion between the same parts of the soul—which
he takes to be the 'parts' discussed in the *Republic*,

reason, passion and desire—though a condition brought
about not through the subjugation of reason by excessive
passion or desire, but through an inability of reason to
function properly: 'a condition in which there is no moral
conflict because the reason has either never possessed
sufficient strength, or has become so weak that one of
the two irrational parts . . . has free play or is at most
hampered by the other'.

It is however possible, and perhaps more likely, that
this disproportion is thought of as primarily a disproportion between soul and body. There is a passage in the
Timaeus (87c ff.) which Hackforth (120) dismisses as
irrelevant to the interpretation of the *Sophist* precisely
because 'the speaker there in fact confines himself to
proportion and disproportion between soul and body,
and says nothing of disproportion *within* the soul'. But
one part of the argument in the *Sophist*, which Hackforth
does not mention, is extremely difficult to understand
except in terms of just such a disproportion between
body and soul.

At *Sophist* 228c, after briefly discussing 'discord and
disease in the soul', the EV says:

But if things which partake of motion and aim at some particular mark pass beside the mark and miss it on every
occasion when they try to hit it, shall we say that this happens
to them through right proportion to one another, or on the
contrary, through disproportion?

'Being ignorant', he goes on to say, 'is simply an aberration (παραφροσύνη) of a soul that aims at truth, when
understanding goes astray' (228c10–d2), and 'a foolish
soul must be put down as ugly and out of proportion'[1]
αἰσχρὰν καὶ ἄμετρον: 228d4).

---

[1] 'Ill-proportioned' (Taylor and Fowler) is a rendering which seems to

Taylor takes the 'things which partake of motion' to be 'moving limbs', which he even incorporates into his translation, although they are not mentioned in the Greek. If this interpretation were correct, the 'moving limbs' would presumably be an analogue for the parts of the soul. But 'things that partake of motion' would be a curious periphrasis for 'moving limbs'; and it would be extremely odd, in an analogy between parts of the body and parts of the soul, to represent limbs as themselves 'aiming at a mark' and 'trying to hit it'. If this were such an analogy, moreover, we should have to admit that it is the *whole* soul which 'aims at truth'. On the other hand, 'things which partake of motion' cannot be intended to *mean* 'the parts of the soul', for there is no definite article; on the contrary, the clause seems to be indefinite.[1] Fowler rightly observes that the reference cannot be to anything like an arrow, because of the remark about 'right proportion *to one another*'.[2]

It would seem that the reference must be to things which *in combination* aim at a mark and miss it, and the passage will make sense if we suppose that the EV is thinking of occasions when *a soul and a body in combination* miss their mark: 'whatever things partaking (in combination) of motion and aiming (in combination) at a mark pass beside it and miss it' must be out of proportion to one another. It is of course the soul, not the body, which does the aiming, and on the present interpretation

assume that the lack of proportion is between the parts of the soul. But the word ἄμετρον need not imply that.

[1] If Cobet's conjecture ὅσ' ἄν for the ὅσα of the manuscripts BT is not accepted, the meaning will still have to be 'all the things which . . .'.

[2] 'The idea,' he says (309, n. 1), 'seems rather to be that moving objects of various sizes, shapes, and rates of speed must interfere with each other.' But apart from other difficulties, if these objects are entirely separate from one another the analogy will not be satisfactory.

we need not suppose that pleasure and desire combine with reason in aiming at truth; for if Plato has in mind a disproportion between soul and body rather than between 'parts of the soul', 'soul' here may be virtually equivalent to 'mind', passion and desire being for the moment regarded, as in the *Timaeus* passage, as belonging to the body.

It is worth quoting from the *Timaeus* to indicate the way Plato thinks of disproportion there. At 87d ff. we read:

The proportion or disproportion between soul and body themselves is more important than any other; yet we . . . fail to perceive or realize that when a great and powerful soul has for its vehicle a frame too small and feeble, or again when the two are ill-matched in the contrary way, the creature as a whole is not beautiful, since it is deficient in the most important proportions. . . . When the soul in it is too strong for the body and of ardent temperament, she dislocates the whole frame and fills it with ailments from within. . . . When a large body, too big for the soul, is conjoined with a small and feeble mind, whereas the appetites natural to man are of two kinds—desire of food for the body and desire of wisdom for the divinest part in us—the motions of the stronger part prevail and, by augmenting their own power while they make the powers of the soul dull and slow to learn and forgetful, they produce in her the worst of maladies, stupidity (ἀμαθία).

The term 'stupidity' (ἀμαθία) is used here and elsewhere in the *Timaeus* not with the narrow reference given to it in the *Sophist*, but for what the *Sophist* calls 'ignorance' (ἄγνοια).[1]

If we suppose that Plato is thinking in comparable

[1] Likewise the term 'madness' (μανία) is seemingly used in reference to

terms of a disproportion between soul and body in the *Sophist*, certain difficulties are, as we have seen, removed or at least attenuated. No doubt a disproportion of this sort would also mean that, within the soul, reason was out of proportion to passion and desire. But if Plato has in mind trouble due in the first instance to feebleness or aberration of the mind, and not to a general disharmony between a multiplicity of 'parts', it is appropriate that he should put the emphasis, as in the *Timaeus*, on the simpler relationship between body and soul.

The question arises whether such a disproportion would necessarily mean that reason lost its supremacy, and passion and/or desire had partial or complete control. The *Timaeus* passage might suggest that it would. If so, the general effect would normally be the same as the effect of 'discord', though the original cause would be different.[1] But it may be that Plato is quite as much concerned with cases where the reason is weak, but not submerged.[2] Certainly ignorance may sometimes exist 'only in the soul' (228d), and we are told, apparently as a generalization, that ignorance is an aberration of the soul and that a foolish soul is ugly and out of proportion (228c–d); and again, quite explicitly, that *all* ignorance calls for instruction (229a). If ignorance that is 'only in

what the *Sophist* calls 'wickedness' (πονηρία), and 'diseases' (νόσοι) is the generic term, not 'evils' (κακά).

[1] Hackforth (see above, p. 47f.) clearly assumes that a disproportion between parts of the soul would have this result. The case of which he writes, where the reason is so weak that there is 'no moral conflict' at all, would be an extreme case. Normally, despite its measure of weakness and ignorance, one might expect that the reason would not accept the dictates of passion or desire without putting up a fight, even though it had lost control: there would be some sort of conflict.

[2] In the *Timaeus* passage (87d ff.: above, p. 50) the rendering 'prevail' is perhaps too strong. The Greek (κρατοῦσα) may mean no more than 'acquire power'. In any case we need not suppose that the *Timaeus* doctrine must apply here in all its detail.

the soul' implies a lack of proportion, but is still something that is not popularly regarded as an evil, it must be
possible to have such a disproportion without *domination*
of reason by passion and/or desire. These 'motions of the
stronger part' (i.e. of the body), as the *Timaeus* passage
calls them, will then be stronger, in relation to the mind,
than is desirable, but still not supreme. Indeed, it might
happen that their functioning and that of the mind came
close to being in a state of what the *Republic* calls justice,
even though the philosophically desirable proportion
between body and mind had not been attained—the
reason being too weak and too much preoccupied with
keeping passion and desire in their proper places to
achieve true wisdom. We cannot be sure that Plato has
such cases in mind, but he might well consider them
more likely than others to respond to treatment by
appropriate instruction.

4. THE FIRST SIX SERIES OF DIVISIONS

There is one last, minor point concerning the first six
series of Divisions that needs to be considered. It is not
easy to decide whether they are supposed to present
different aspects of sophistry (so Taylor, *Plato*, 379), or to
describe different types of sophist. The question is not of
great importance, for even if we are concerned with
aspects of sophistry, some sophists will have emphasized
and represented some aspects more than others. But we
may note that series 2, 3 and 4 will reach definitions that
are mutually incompatible (see the appendix to this
chapter), and that although they could have been reduced
to a single series by omitting all question of the manner
of selling, the EV has preferred to treat them as distinct

(231d). Again, whereas series 1–5 seem to limit the subject-matter with which the sophist deals to excellence (ἀρετή), the EV later recognizes (232c–e) that sophists deal with many other matters besides, in fact with 'all things' (232e, 233c). Probably, therefore, we should conclude that the first six series are attempts at defining particular kinds of sophist. If so, we may say with Cornford (187) that these six earlier series are in effect a Collection made in preparation for the seventh, which is concerned only with what is essential to all sophists. This latter view, which is hardly tenable on Cornford's own supposition that the sixth series 'does not define any type of Sophist' (173) and is introduced simply because Socrates was someone 'to whom the name had been attached' (187), is quite compatible with the present interpretation of that series.

The first six series are summarized at 231c–e, and there then follows a discussion leading to the choice of a new genus, Image-making. This provides the occasion for an important discussion concerning meanings of 'is' and 'is not' and relationships between Forms, and the final definition is not reached until the end of the dialogue.

APPENDIX

The Divisions are presented here diagrammatically for easy reference, except for the third and fourth series on the Sophist, which are not reconstructed here. Plato does not present them systematically, but in brief summary and as variations on the theme of the second series. The EV states in somewhat vague terms at 224d–e that the name sophistry will also be given to 'whatever branch of the knowledge trade there is, in both the retail and own product marketing sections, that deals with this type of subject'. It appears that parallel sets of Divisions to those based on inter-city merchandising in the second series can be constructed on two of the left-hand members of that series, leading to Sophistry by alternative routes. (In the numbering at 224d and 225e these are in fact presented as a single alternative jointly forming the third series, but they are distinguished at 231d and given the numbering 3 and 4 adopted here.)

Angling is used not only as a general paradigm of the method of Division, but to provide a platform for the first five series on the Sophist (see above). The sixth series starts from a third major division of Art, namely the Art of separation, but the others all take some part of the Angling series for granted, as indicated in the diagram.

The seventh series suggests that Division may be a more complex process than Plato seems normally to envisage. Such phrases as 'the right-hand section' (264e) indicate the usual two-dimensional genealogical pattern, but at 266a the EV states that the Art of production can be divided both across the width and along the length. To get a complete picture of the main species of the art, two parameters are required, the divine–human axis and the object–image axis. Similar problems could arise elsewhere in these series of Divisions (e.g. 224d–e, 228a), but it is only here that there is any explicit indication that the two-dimensional pattern is not adequate. An attempt is made to show this feature in the diagram. (This is of course a different problem from the question whether a class may be divided into more than two subdivisions on a single parameter, a licence which would perhaps have been useful at 220a–b to allow a straightforward three-fold Division of living things.)

ANGLING: 219a-221c

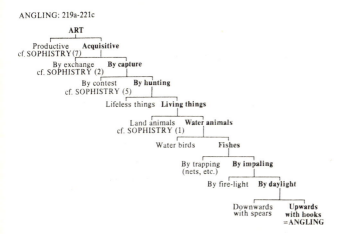

SOPHISTRY (1): 221c-223b

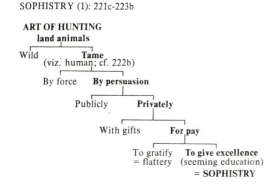

SOPHISTRY (2): 223c-224c

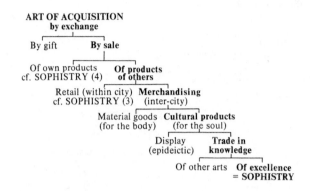

ART OF ACQUISITION
by exchange

By gift   **By sale**

Of own products   **Of products**
cf. SOPHISTRY (4)   **of others**

Retail (within city)   **Merchandising**
cf. SOPHISTRY (3)   (inter-city)

Material goods   **Cultural products**
(for the body)   (for the soul)

Display   **Trade in**
(epideictic) **knowledge**

Of other arts **Of excellence**
    = **SOPHISTRY**

SOPHISTRY (3) and (4): 224d-e
Parallel series based on members of the second series (see above).

SOPHISTRY (5): 224e-226a

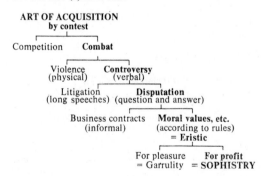

ART OF ACQUISITION
by contest

Competition   **Combat**

Violence   **Controversy**
(physical)   (verbal)

Litigation   **Disputation**
(long speeches) (question and answer)

Business contracts   **Moral values, etc.**
(informal)   (according to rules)
    = **Eristic**

For pleasure   **For profit**
= Garrulity = **SOPHISTRY**

SOPHISTRY (6): 226a-231b

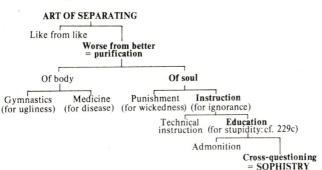

ART OF SEPARATING

Like from like

**Worse from better
= purification**

Of body

Gymnastics (for ugliness)   Medicine (for disease)

Of soul

Punishment (for wickedness)   **Instruction** (for ignorance)

Technical instruction   **Education** (for stupidity: cf. 229c)

Admonition

**Cross-questioning
= SOPHISTRY**

SOPHISTRY (7): 265a-268d (cf. 235b-236d)

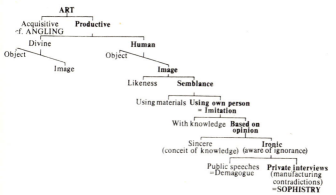

ART

Acquisitive cf. ANGLING   **Productive**

Divine

Object   Image

Human

Object   **Image**

Likeness   **Semblance**

Using materials   **Using own person
= Imitation**

With knowledge   **Based on opinion**

Sincere (conceit of knowledge)   **Ironic** (aware of ignorance)

Public speeches =Demagogue   **Private interviews** (manufacturing contradictions)
=SOPHISTRY

IMAGES AND 'WHAT IS NOT'

I. THE GENUS IMAGE-MAKING

The EV recalls that the Sophist has appeared to be a kind of hunter, a kind of merchant, a kind of retailer, a kind of seller of his own products, a kind of disputant, and a kind of purger of opinions that obstruct learning. He suggests (232a) that when someone is known by the name of a single art but yet appears to be master of many, there must be something wrong with this appearance. There is probably a hint here, in the word 'appearance' (φάντ-ασμα), that all the kinds of knowledge which the Sophist seems to possess are only appearances; and we are perhaps meant to be reminded of *Republic* x (598c–d), where we find that anyone supposed to have knowledge in a great variety of matters must be suspect. But all that the EV explicitly infers is that we have yet to discover the essential principle behind all the skills that have been attributed to the Sophist.

The Sophist was particularly well described, says the EV, as a disputant, and he disputes and teaches others to dispute about a variety of subjects; indeed, the art of disputation seems to be a capacity to dispute about anything; but it is surely not possible for a man to know everything, and a man who is ignorant can hardly say anything sound when he controverts someone who knows (233a). Yet the Sophist creates in his pupils the belief that he is wise in all things. He appears to be wise, but is not; he is believed to be wise, but is not; he has seeming knowledge which is not genuine (οὐκ ἀλήθειαν, 233c).

Underlying this 'marvel' (θαῦμα, 233a), as we soon see,
is the problem of explaining the nature of false appearances and of false belief. He has the art, says the EV, of
producing 'images in speech' (εἴδωλα λεγόμενα, 234c)
that have the appearance of truth but in fact are deceptive, just as an artist may deceive by creating in his draw-
ings the illusion of real things. But not all speech is
deceptive, and even true statements can do no more,
in Plato's view, than image-forth reality (cf. *Letter* VII.
342a-3d; Bluck, *Phaedo*, 113, n. 3; 167, n. 1); and it is no
doubt for this reason that the EV is made to divide
Image-making into Likeness-making (εἰκαστική) and
Semblance-making (φανταστική) (235d-236c; see the discussion in Gulley, p. 149 f.). The example that he gives
of Likeness-making is drawn from sculpture: 'creating a
copy that conforms to the proportions of the original in
all three dimensions and giving moreover the proper
colour to every part'. Semblance-making, on the other
hand, is the creation of an image that only *seems* to
resemble the original, as the result of deliberate illusion,
as when sculptors or painters take into account perspec-
tive rather than true proportions.

It is always dangerous to press Plato's analogies
farther than the context requires, and it is unnecessary to
assume here that all semblances are thought of, like the
paintings of *Republic* x, as being at two removes from
reality, or that we are meant to detect an ontological
difference between a likeness and a semblance. Cornford
(198 f.) supposes that semblances 'imply two relations
between image and original' and are 'conceived as
possessing in some sense a *lower grade of reality*' (Cornford's
italics), whereas a likeness is 'a reproduction or replica,
such as the making of a second actual bed'. But there is

no reason to suppose, as Cornford does, that Plato is here using the term 'likeness' 'in a narrower sense than usual', and that he would no longer think of a 'likeness' of X, as he does in the *Cratylus*, as something to be contrasted with a 'replica' of X, a second X. Even likenesses are represented as no more than a species of images, and we may infer from 235e that the EV would describe *some* works of sculpture and painting as 'likenesses'. Semblances differ from these in that they involve an element of deliberate illusion, and if we may regard the distinction as having been introduced solely in order to emphasize the falsity of what the Sophist says, we are not here in any way concerned with degrees of reality, but only with the question whether images—and falsehood—exist at all.

The EV cannot decide whether the Sophist is a Likeness-maker or a Semblance-maker (236c), because, as he says, the Sophist has taken refuge in a class (εἶδος) which baffles investigation. This should be taken to mean that the genus Image-making as a whole is baffling;[1] even 'true likenesses' involve the difficulty that although they are 'like' their originals, they are not genuine: they 'are not' those originals (240b). No doubt the EV feels that the Sophist belongs to Semblance-making, and made his division because of the Sophist's deceptiveness, as we have seen. But one can hardly maintain that he must belong to the one species rather than to the other of the puzzling genus Image-making, unless 'appearing' without 'being' and falsehood itself can be explained. For to say or think, for example, that falsity really 'is' is to say or think that 'what is not' *is*, and Parmenides

[1] Cf. 239c–d, where in virtually repeating his present remark the EV says: 'Let us say that the Sophist has found an impenetrable lurking-place. . . . When we call him an image-maker, he will ask what on earth we mean in speaking of an image at all.'

declared that 'what is not' cannot 'be' (237a). The claim that one can say or think 'what is not' must therefore be tested.

2. 'WHAT IS NOT' AS 'WHAT HAS NO BEING'

The EV begins by (in effect) treating 'what is not' as equivalent to 'what has no being' and maintaining in three brief arguments that nothing at all can be said about it.

(a) *237b7–e7*. The expression cannot be applied to what is, and therefore it cannot be applied to a thing (τι), since 'a thing' (τι) is used only of what is: so that he who talks about 'what is not' must be talking about nothing (μηδὲν λέγειν). Here μηδὲν λέγειν is ambiguous, as it can mean either 'to talk about nothing' or 'to talk nonsense'. No doubt the ambiguity is intentional, the implication being that to talk about nothing is to talk nonsense.[1] The EV's next remark involves yet a third possible meaning of μηδὲν λέγειν, 'to say nothing'. It will not even do, he says, to assert that he who talks about 'what is not' is talking but talking about (or saying) nothing (λέγειν μηδέν): we must say that he is not talking at all (οὐδὲ λέγειν).

We cannot be sure what Plato would have said about the possible retort that we can and do talk about mermaids and other imaginary composite creatures. But (to judge from what is said about the Chimaera, Scylla and Cerberus at *Republic* 588c–d) he might have claimed that

---

[1] As Cornford (205) says, 'the ambiguity does not vitiate the argument'. Plato not infrequently makes use of double meanings, to stress the point that he wishes to make.

what we are really talking about are the *parts* (girl and tail, for example) which do correspond, severally, to real things. What we cannot talk about are things which do not correspond to what exists in any way at all. We may try to formulate general propositions about such things as a class; but we cannot say anything about a particular thing which neither as a whole nor in its parts corresponds to what exists. We can put together words each of which severally has its referent, and even give a name to what we allege the resulting formula denotes—e.g. girl and tail = mermaid; the present king of France = Napoleon X. We may imagine a new species of plant or animal, and describe it in terms of genus and specific difference. But in all these cases it could be said that what we are really talking about is not the one non-existent thing we are trying to talk about, but the several existent things in terms of which we are formulating descriptions.

It might still be argued that these are nevertheless descriptions of things that do not exist. To this the answer of the argument is that only what is something can be described, and what is something must exist. Such 'descriptions' have indeed no referent, but 'things that do not exist' is a contradiction in terms.

The argument is perhaps easier to grasp, though not materially altered, if we may assume that Plato assimilated to each other the existential and the copulative senses of 'to be', that both for him are embraced by the term 'being', and that 'what is not' here means 'what does not exist *or have any character* (οὐσία)'. To talk about what has no character at all would indeed be to talk about nothing; in fact, if one tried to talk about 'it' one would be reduced to silence. That Plato should have assimilated these two senses of 'to be' is explicable if he assumed that what exists must have or be a character, and that what has or is a character must exist—that essence and existence go together; and that he is here assimilating them is suggested not only by the fact that he clearly does so later on,[1] but also by the third of the present three arguments, to which we shall come in a moment.

(b) *238a5–c11*. To that which is not, nothing that is can belong. But we cannot mention or conceive of a thing that is not or things that are not without by implication making an attribution of singular or plural number; and number is a thing that is. Therefore 'what is not' is unmentionable and inconceivable.

Mermaids of course are conceivable and mentionable, but here again what we are thinking of is 'girl' and 'tail'. 'What is not' is not even a thing, and therefore quite inconceivable. And if 'what is not' *means* 'what does not exist or have any character', then to assign any attribute to it would be absurd; but since we cannot think of it or mention it without doing so, it is clearly inconceivable and unmentionable.

Moravcsik (26) strangely remarks, 'A non-existent, or a group of non-existents, is inconceivable. From this is it concluded that Non-existence itself is inconceivable.' But τὸ μὴ ὂν αὐτὸ καθ' αὑτό (238c9) undoubtedly means simply 'that which is not' all by itself, without any properties—not the *concept* of being non-existent (and/or characterless).

(c) *238d4–239b3*. From what has been said, it follows that even to try to deny that 'what is not' can 'be' involves self-contradiction. Thus the EV, in asserting that 'what is not'

---

[1] See pp. 67f., 118f., 147f., 158, n. 2.

is unmentionable (238c10), has contradicted his former assertions by attaching 'to be' (εἶναι) to it; and he has himself referred to it as though it were singular in number. So nothing can be said of it.

Now the 'being' that the EV has attached to 'what is not' by describing it as unmentionable is not simply existence. He has attributed to it a particular attribute, 'being such-and-such'. Since 'being' must therefore correspond to or include the copulative, characterizing sense of 'to be', 'what is not' should probably be taken to mean 'what does not exist or have any character'. This accords with what we shall find in a later part of the discussion.[1]

Moravcsik (27) takes the conclusion of this argument too to be concerned with the concept of non-existence; and in a general comment on the three arguments he writes: 'The conclusion that "non-existence" is meaningless (and the ensuing perplexities) could have been avoided had Plato not used the fact that Non-existence cannot have an extension to infer the impossibility of the concept itself.' But there is no evidence that any such inference has been drawn.

From these arguments the EV concludes (239c) that until someone can say something correctly about 'what is not', without attributing to it being or singularity or plurality, the Sophist must be admitted to have hidden himself in an inexplorable hiding-place. Later, at 258e, the EV alludes to this conclusion when he says, 'Let no one say that it is the opposite of "what is" to which we refer when we make bold to assert that "what is not" is. We have long ago dismissed the question whether or not there is anything opposed to "what is", whether any account can be given of it or none whatsoever.' Plato,

[1] For references see p. 63 n.

we may suppose, really believed that nothing can be said about 'a thing that is not'. The EV's arguments have explained the assertion at 236d that the Sophist has taken refuge in a class (image-makers) that baffles investigation, and this assertion has now been virtually repeated (239c). If charged with being an image-maker, the Sophist can always retort by asking what is meant by an image (239d). The difficulty involved is brought out in 240a–c.

Theaet. Well, Stranger, what could we say an image was, except another such thing, fashioned in the likeness of the genuine thing?

EV. Do you mean another such genuine thing, or what do you mean by 'such'?

Theaet. Certainly not genuine, but something like it.

EV. Meaning by 'genuine' what *really is*?

Theaet. Yes.

EV. Well, what is not genuine is the opposite of genuine?

Theaet. Of course.

EV. So if you say that what is *like* is not genuine, you say that it *is not, having no reality.*[1]

---

[1] The text here (240b7) would appear to be οὐκ ὄντως οὐκ ὂν ἄρα λέγεις τὸ ἐοικός. Runciman (68) points out that this reading is well attested, and would take οὐκ ὄντως οὐκ ὄν to mean 'not really non-existent'. 'The argument', he says, 'must then be that a likeness is neither a real thing (240b2) nor a really unreal thing; that is to say, not to be assigned to the class of τὸ μηδαμῶς ὄν discussed in the preceding argument'. (See also Kohnke, 37 ff.) But the EV's present utterance is a deduction (n. b. the ἄρα, 'so') from the previous admissions, and must mean that a likeness *is not.*

Cornford (211, n. 1) notes that Diès and Friedländer would understand these words here and οὐκ ὂν οὐκ ὄντως (b12) 'as a "complete negation" of ὄντως ὄν: *"un irréel non-être"* ', but adds: 'This is impossible Greek and also the wrong sense. An *eidolon* is not the complete negation of ὄντως ὄν (which is τὸ μηδαμῶς ὄν), but is an ὄν, only not ὄντως but πως.' This objection arises largely out of Cornford's preconception that we have to do with gradational ontology. The EV is explaining the possible retort of the Sophist, according to which an image would seem to be the opposite of ὄντως ὄν. The Greek is odd, but perhaps acceptable if we suppose that the EV has (illogically) negatived both words for emphasis. Cornford and Taylor follow Burnet in excising the second οὐκ both here and in b12.

Theaet. And yet it has being in a way.

EV. But not *genuine* being, you say.

Theaet. No, indeed—except that it really is a likeness.

EV. So although it is not, having no reality, it really is what we call a likeness?

Theaet. What is not does seem to be combined with what is in some such way. It is very strange.

This passage has been variously interpreted, but the difficulty here discussed, the difficulty that would face those who wanted to substantiate the charge that the Sophist was an image-maker, is simply this: if an image *is not* (identical with) the thing imaged, it might appear to have *no being at all*, and yet if it really is an image, it must really 'be'. The solution which the EV eventually finds is to isolate the 'is' which expresses identity, and then to show that 'is not' can express non-identity, meaning 'is other than'.[1] The conclusion is not, as Cornford (210) says, that we must 'recognize a third intermediate region of things that are neither wholly real nor utterly non-existent'. We are not concerned with degrees of reality.[2] The only question here is how a thing that 'is not' something else can 'be' at all—how it can even 'be' itself.

---

[1] See p. 99, 106, 113f., 134ff., 141f., 151, 161f.

[2] Runciman (69) thinks that ἔστι πως ('has being in a way') will have to mean that a likeness exists only 'to some (limited) extent', because the EV's reply shows that it may be contrasted with ἀληθῶς (ἔστι), 'genuine being'. (Runciman's ἀληθινῶς must be a misprint.) But the contrast is *forced* upon Theaetetus, who may simply have meant that a likeness must have being somehow. Theaetetus' 'No, indeed', accepting the EV's remark, is probably due to bewilderment, but could be due to his taking the EV to mean that the likeness does not have its being *as the genuine article,* i.e. it is not the genuine original. The catch lies in the ambiguity of ἀληθῶς. But in any case the 'contrast' affords no evidence to settle this particular question.

Cornford (211, n. 1) seems to take ὄντως ὄν to mean 'really existent' as opposed to ὄν πως, 'having some sort of existence' (a lesser degree of reality). But ὄντως is used in the EV's remark at b12 'it *really* is a *likeness*'.

There is a further difficulty. The 'semblance' which the Sophist was said to create instils in us false opinion. But false opinion will be thinking things that are not (240d). If, therefore, we insist that falsity exists, we are forced to attribute being to what is not (241a–b). To counter such a retort, says the EV, it will in fact be necessary somehow to refute Parmenides' pronouncement, and to establish that what is not, in some respect is, and that what is, in a way is not (241d).

Obviously if this is to be achieved, it can only be done by giving to 'what is not' a sense other than the one that has been given to it in this section. It is in fact achieved by giving it the sense 'what is other': everything may be said to be the same as itself and to have being, but at the same time not to be (to be other than) all other things. Thus false statement and false belief are not talking or thinking about nothing. They are concerned with things that are not the appropriate things, but are nevertheless 'things that are'.

Lastly, it may be remarked here that although Plato very clearly sets out to distinguish the identitative sense of 'to be', it is not apparently his purpose to distinguish the existential sense from the copula. We have already had some slight indication of this in the argument that to say that 'what is not' '*is* unmentionable' is to attach 'being' to it (238d–239b). There is perhaps a further slight indication of it in the argument at 240b: whereas a likeness might appear *not to be* (since it 'is not' the original), this is paradoxical not, be it noted, because likenesses manifestly do exist, but because a likeness 'really *is* (has the character of being) a likeness'. Other and clearer indications will appear later on.[1] But the point may be

---

[1] For references see p. 63 n. above.

made here because those who think that Plato does distinguish the existential 'is' from the copula often base their belief on a false (or at best a dubious) interpretation of the present section.

Plato shows in the *Sophist*, they argue, that to say 'what is not' is not to talk about what is *non-existent*, but to talk about what *is not X*, and this is tantamount to distinguishing the copula from the existential 'is'. But it looks in fact as though Plato has not differentiated non-existence from characterlessness. His point here is rather that it is impossible to talk about 'what is not' (as the opposite of 'what is') precisely because it 'is not' *anything*, i.e. *has no character* at all. In other words, the predicative sense of 'is' is as clearly present here as it is in the later elucidation of 'what is not' as 'what is other than *X*'. There is therefore no justification for seeing any distinction between copula and existential 'is' implicit in the contrast Plato actually draws between the usages of 'what is not'.

3. CONCLUSION

In order to define the Sophist it is necessary to show how an image can *not be* (identical with) the thing imaged, and yet *be*, and also to show that to think things that are not can in fact be to think something, since one sense of 'what is not' reduces us to silence. To achieve this purpose the EV must disprove Parmenides' famous dictum and show that what is not, in some respect is, and that what is, in a way is not.

CHAPTER III: 242b–245e

VIEWS ABOUT 'WHAT IS'—
PLURALISTS AND MONISTS

I. PLURALISTS

The EV approaches the task of refuting Parmenides'
pronouncement by considering the nature of 'what is'.
It is suggested that although this is something about
which we are supposed to be quite clear, we may in fact
be in some confusion about it, as we are about 'what is
not' (243b7–c5); and at 246a we shall find that 'what is'
is as hard to define as 'what is not'. Later, at 250e, the
EV remarks that since both are equally puzzling, 'there
is henceforth some hope that any light thrown upon the
one will illuminate the other to an equal degree'. The
puzzlement, as we shall see, is not long afterwards dis-
solved, by the isolation of the identitative sense of 'is'
and the demonstration that 'is not' can mean 'is other
than'.[1] But the immediate aim is to show that Being (the
concept, or 'thing' as Plato would call it, that corresponds to the meaning of the existential and/or characterizing 'is') is something different from anything which
philosophers have described as 'what is'.

The EV considers the theories of those who have tried
to determine 'how many real things there are' (242c),
beginning with the pluralists—not necessarily materialists,
as Moravcsik (29) has pointed out, but anyone who
posited more than one real thing (244b1–4). Those, for
example, who say that Hot and Cold are the totality of

[1] For references see p. 66, n. 1.

things should explain what they mean by the word 'are' (τὸ εἶναι) (243d–4a):

Are we to postulate that this is a third thing apart from those two, and suppose that according to you the totality is no longer two things, but three? For presumably you do not call one of the two Being,[1] and then say that both equally are; for then in both cases [i.e. whether you identify Being with the Hot *or* with the Cold] they would pretty certainly be one and not two. . . . Do you want then to call the two together 'Being'? . . . But that too, my friends, we shall say, would clearly be speaking of the two things as one.

The EV is assuming that the term 'are' (or 'to be') must refer to some real thing. He seems to suggest that even the dualists would be unable to deny this. If, therefore, they wish to maintain their thesis that Hot and Cold are the only 'things' there are, they must identify Being with one or the other, or with the two combined. But if they identify it with one only of the two, the other of the two cannot be said to *be*; for if Being is identified with Hot, for example, then to say 'Cold is' will be identical with saying 'Cold is hot', which is absurd, because Hot and Cold are *ex hypothesi* 'things' whose characters are opposed to one another. It may be thought that this interpretation of the first part of the argument reads more into the EV's words than could have been intended, but it is supported by a similar argument at 250a–b, to which we come presently.[2] Again, if our dualists identify

---

[1] The Greek (καλοῦντες θάτερον ὄν) is ambiguous as between 'designating one of the two "Being" ' and 'describing one of the two as having being', but the context clearly requires the sense of identification with Being.

[2] See p. 103ff. Cornford (220) and Taylor (38–9) give similar interpretations. Moravcsik (29) says that if 'Existence' is identical with one of the two, 'then Existence does not apply to these two in the same sense ("ὁμοίως", 243e5)'. But if it is the name of one, this by itself is no proof that it could not also be applied to both in the same sense, so that there is

Being with both Hot and Cold, they will be treating
Hot-and-Cold as one thing, not as two.

Moravcsik (29) objects that this part of the argument
'will not suffice' to show that 'theories of this kind do not
explain Existence', for 'as it stands it is a general protest
against disjunctive definitions' and 'it would not convince
those who find such definitions acceptable'. It is difficult
to be sure what he has in mind, but presumably he is
thinking of some such definition as this: 'A thing *is* if and
only if it is either hot or cold.' But though this might
'explain Existence', it does not absolve the dualists of
unwittingly treating Existence (or Being) as a 'third
thing'; for such a definition will not allow us to *equate* it—
the concept—with either or with both. 'Being' here
(τὸ εἶναι) does not mean the sum of all that is; it is something that corresponds to the meaning of 'is' or 'are'; and
hence it is a single thing. For this reason, whatever it is
equated with must likewise be a single thing. Hence, if it
is to be equated with Hot and Cold, Hot-and-Cold must
be a single thing, which is absurd.[1] The objection to the
pluralists is that, however many things they have said
'are', they always failed to treat Being (as they should
have done) as a separate, additional entity.

Moravcsik seems to have been misled by the notion
that Plato is arguing that 'Existence cannot be defined
in terms of a set of concepts' (28). Plato's object is not to
prove that 'Existence is undefinable', but to show that it

no advantage in taking ὁμοίως in this way. In any case, the objection
contained in the following sentence, that the two would consequently
be reduced to one, makes no sense on this interpretation.

[1] The point is not that there will be 'one real thing (composed of two
parts)' (Cornford 220), for the meaning of 'is' does not have two parts.
Nor is the point likely to be that if Being is equated with Hot and Cold,
those two must be identical with each other (Taylor *ad loc.*). τὰ ἄμφω will
mean 'the pair jointly'.

cannot be identified or equated with the things that philosophers have described as *being*. Moravcsik also remarks (29) that Plato is 'attempting to refute those who would identify Existence with a plurality of concepts'. But the pluralists have not tried to identify Existence (or Being) with the things that they have claimed 'are'; they have simply left it out of account. And it is Plato's argument that they could not successfully defend their several theses even if they tried to identify it with any or all of their 'things that are'.

2. MONISTS

Next the EV turns to 'all those who say that the All is one thing' (244b),[1] and considers what they may mean by 'what is' (τὸ ὄν). If they describe as 'being' (ὄν: i.e. as what *is*) the same thing as they describe as 'one', they seem to be applying two names to one thing. But (i) when they say that there is only one thing, they can hardly say that there are two names (the objection is not to their calling one thing by two names, but to their saying, while ostensibly monists, that there are two of anything); and (ii) it is equally absurd to allow that there is such a thing as a name, since 'it could not explain itself':[2] for if the name is different from the thing it designates, then these are two entities; and if the name is the same as the thing, then either it is not the name of anything or it is the name of something which is itself a name.

---

[1] Not only Parmenides and the Eleatics, probably, though no doubt he is thinking primarily of them. See p. 82.

[2] This must be the meaning of λόγον οὐκ ἂν ἔχον. The participle must agree with ὄνομα. Taylor and Fowler translate as though the text had ἔχοι, Cornford (221) as though ἔχον somehow agreed with the whole ὡς clause ('it is equally absurd to allow anyone to assert that a name can have any existence, when that would be inexplicable').

This argument does not necessarily assume, as Moravcsik (31) supposes, that terms exist in the same sense as
the things which they designate. It is enough for the
purpose of the argument that 'are' can be applied to
names and *designata* alike: they both have some sort of
being. Nor does the argument presuppose, as Cornford
(220) imagines, Plato's own view that names refer to
Forms. It simply suggests that if names exist they must
designate things other than themselves, and that the
monists have overlooked what our use of names implies.[1]

There follows (244d-245d) what has sometimes been
treated as an entirely separate argument against the
monists (e.g. Moravcsik, 31; Runciman, 74), but in fact
is better regarded as simply a continuation or second
part of a single argument. Misunderstanding has arisen
probably as a result of the assumption that the EV is
talking about Unity, Wholeness and Being (or Existence), whereas in fact he is continuing to talk about the
terms or 'names' used in reference to what the monists
regarded as real—'being' (or 'what is'), 'the one' and
'the whole'.[2] The first two have already been mentioned.
He now introduces the third. The passage may be

---

[1] Parmenides, of course, might have defended himself by asserting
that his 'one' cannot properly be described or designated at all. But
Plato is anxious to take a common-sense view of the matter, and assumes
that his monists do allow (however inadvertently) that there are such
things as names. Not to do so would in any case cast serious doubt on the
significance of their doctrine. [Crombie (vol. II, p. 393) takes the difficulty
more seriously, arguing that Parmenides would regard names as 'appearance' and therefore no more fatal to monism than 'mice, thunderstorms
and so on'. Unfortunately the interpretation which he offers to protect
Plato's argument from this attack is unconvincing. It involves a highly
forced sense of 'name' (ὄνομα), and an impossible exegesis of Plato's
point about the impossibility of using even a single name of 'the one'.]
[2] The monists may not have used these expressions as what we would
call names, though Parmenides in his poem uses all three epithets.

translated thus (somewhat literally, to avoid begging any questions):[1]

EV. What about 'the whole'? Will they say that it is other than 'the one that is'[2] or the same?

Theaet. Of course they will and do say it is the same.

EV. Then if it is a whole, as Parmenides says, 'every way like the mass of a well-rounded sphere', . . . it must certainly have parts. . . . Now there is no reason why what is divided into parts should not have been affected by 'the one' (πάθος τοῦ ἑνὸς ἔχειν)[3] in respect of its parts considered all together, and in this way be one, as being a sum or whole. . . . But what has been affected in this way (τὸ πεπονθὸς ταῦτα)[4] cannot itself be 'the one' itself. . . . The genuine 'one' must be affirmed, on a correct account, to be altogether without parts. . . . But such a thing as this, being composed of many parts, will not fit that account (244d–245b). . . . Then (i) will 'what is' have been affected by 'the one' and in this way be 'one' and 'whole', or (ii) are we to deny utterly that 'what is' is a whole?[5] . . . For (i) although 'what is' has been so affected as to be 'one' in a way, it will be seen not to be the same thing as 'the one', and the sum of things will be more than one (245b4–9). . . . But again, (ii) if it is not the case that 'what is' is a whole through having been affected by that character [by 'the one', i.e. if

[1] For further discussion of particular points in the passage see the appendix to this chapter. (There are two minor omissions in the translation in the fourth sentence and one at 245b7, but apart from that only replies by Theaetetus have been left out.)

[2] τοῦ ὄντος ἑνός, i.e. 'the one' and 'what is', which (as we have seen) they treat as being identical with each other.

[3] This may seem a strange way of saying 'having the property of unity', but the EV is arguing so far as possible within the framework of the monists' own doctrine—which is difficult when he wants to refer to the possession of a property. See appendix to this chapter.

[4] Or possibly, 'in these ways', but see appendix to this chapter, p. 88.

[5] So with the reading of Schleiermacher, adopted by Cornford and Taylor. The reading of the manuscripts gives 'that "the whole" is a whole'.

it is not a unified whole],[1] but (a) 'the whole' itself exists, then 'what is' turns out to fall short of itself. . . . And so on this reasoning 'what is', being deprived of itself, will 'not be' (οὐκ ὂν ἔσται τὸ ὄν)[1]. . . . And moreover the sum of things is more than one, since 'what is' and 'the whole' have each acquired their own separate natures[1] (245c1–9) . . . . But if (b) 'the whole' does not exist at all, this same conclusion [i.e. that it does not exist][1] attaches to 'what is' (ταὐτὰ ταῦτα ὑπάρχει τῷ ὄντι), and there also attaches to it, in addition to not being, the result that it could never even have become a thing that is. . . . What has come into being has always come into being as a whole, so that if you do not count ['the one' or][2] 'the whole' among the things that are, you have no right to speak of being (οὐσία) or coming-into-being as existing. . . . Again, what is not a whole cannot even be of any definite number, for whatever is of a definite number must amount to that number, whatever it may be, as a whole. (245c11–d10)

First it is necessary to consider interpretations which assume that the EV is talking about Unity and Wholeness.

Moravcsik speaks of 'the One' and 'the Whole', but it is clear from his interpretation that he takes these to be the concepts Unity and Wholeness. Holding (28) that throughout this part of the dialogue Plato is trying 'to establish his own account of Existence', he writes (30):

Parmenides described reality as existing, as a whole, and as unitary, and yet he also maintained that reality is characterized by only one attribute. This position could be maintained consistently only if one were to say that Existence, the One, and the Whole are identical with each other. Plato shows Parmenides to be inconsistent by disproving this

[1] Cf. appendix to this chapter.
[2] These words (τὸ ἓν ἤ) appear in the manuscripts BT but are excised by Bekker. They seem irrelevant here, and may have been inserted in view of 245b4. See further p. 81, n. 3.

identification. In doing this he also establishes that Existence is not identical with either the One or the Whole. His conclusion that Existence has its own nature (245c9) goes beyond what is required to refute Parmenides, and supports the claim that Existence is an indefinable concept. The One and the Whole are all-inclusive topic-neutral concepts. They are the likeliest candidates for identification with Existence. In establishing their separateness from Existence Plato does as much as he can to show the indefinability of Existence.

Moravcsik takes the argument to be in two halves, and the first half (down to 245b9) to 'show a contrast between the meanings of "to exist" and "to be one" '. But it is awkward to take τὸ ἕν as meaning Unity in 245a, when in 244d it was used of the 'name' or description applied to the monists' 'what is'. Moreover τὸ ὄν was similarly used at 244b, and is certainly still so used at 245b; for it would be absurd to consider even for a moment that the concept of Existence might not only be extended in space, but also have spatially distinguishable parts. But if τὸ ὄν is 'what is', τὸ ἕν is far more likely to be 'the one' (of the monists) than Unity, with which it would be odd even to consider identifying 'what is'.[1]

The 'second half' of the argument is taken by Moravcsik to establish the separateness of Existence and the Whole (Wholeness). Now in the first place, the subject of 'is' in 244e2 must either be understood from τὸ ὅλον in 244d14, or it must be the thing to which the expressions τὸ ὅλον and τοῦ ὄντος ἑνός are both so dog-

---

[1] Crombie (vol. II, p. 394) similarly refers to 'the property unity conceived of as a named meaning'. Cornford renders τὸ ἀληθῶς ἕν (245a) as 'Unity in the true sense', but it is not clear what 'in the true sense' means, or why it is so certainly without 'parts' (μέρη can mean 'species'). But the Parmenidean 'one' was *ex hypothesi* without parts, though the EV declares this to be impossible. Taylor's rendering 'a veritable unit' misses the point through mistranslating τό.

matically applied by the monists according to Theaetetus. Either view will help to fix the meaning of τὸ ὅλον in 244d14. It is quite clear that we are not talking about Wholeness, which could not be 'like a sphere'; and if τὸ ὅλον does not mean Wholeness here, it is unlikely to in the rest of the argument.[1] But the final proof that it does not have this meaning anywhere in the argument is that there is no reasoning in the text which would justify taking the conclusion at 245c8–9 to be that 'what is'— or Existence—is distinct from Wholeness. Moreover this conclusion is simply something that is found to follow from a hypothesis—that 'what is' is not a whole (245c1)—which the EV himself, as appears from 245d, does not accept.

Moravcsik (33–4) looks for suitable reasoning, and finds some by very curious means. The conclusion that Existence is not identical with Wholeness cannot, he argues, be supposed to follow from the proposition that Existence is something which 'is not' (245c5–6); that proposition is absurd, and one of the premisses from which that followed must be negated; but at 245d4–6, he continues, we find that one of these premisses, that Wholeness exists, is true; therefore the proposition to be negated is the other premiss, that Existence is not a whole, and the proposition that Existence *is* a whole will be the premiss from which the separateness of Existence and Wholeness really follows.

This remarkable *tour de force* is indefensible. From 245c1 onwards the EV has been assuming, for the sake

[1] If the distinction between τὸ ὄν and τὸ ἕν is between 'what is' and 'the one', that between τὸ ὄν and τὸ ὅλον is likely to be between 'what is' and 'the whole'; and *if* the reading of the manuscripts is correct at 245d and τὸ ἕν and τὸ ὅλον are there coupled, it is unlikely that the former is 'the one' but the latter 'Wholeness'.

of the argument, that 'what is' is *not* a whole. It would be
very odd if we were expected not only to draw inferences
for ourselves from argument yet to come (245d4–6),
but to find the required premiss in a hypothesis which
has already been shown to be incompatible with monism
(244e ff.) and is the contradiction of the leading hypothesis of the present section. It may be added that there
is no word here of the assumption that would be crucial
to any such argument, that (as Moravcsik puts it) 'one
thing affecting another cannot be identical with it'. The
notion that if x partakes of Y then x is not identical with
Y is treated as self-evident in the *Parmenides* (158a3–4),
but there is no mention of it here, although there was
every opportunity of mentioning it at 245a–b. We are
told there that a whole of parts may be (copula) one, but
cannot be identical with 'the one'. But we are not told
that it must be distinct because it is 'affected by "the
one"'. We are told that it must be distinct because it has
parts.[1] Furthermore if 245d means, as Moravcsik (34)
says, that 'everything exists as a whole of some sort',
Wholeness itself must be a whole; and in that case it is
even odder that the not-yet-established fact that 'what
is' is a whole should be the ground for distinguishing
'what is' from Wholeness.

  Cornford (222 f.) treats the passage simply as revealing
Parmenides' inconsistency by presenting him with a
dilemma, whether or not 'the Real' is a whole of parts.
He takes it that in considering the possibility that the
Real is not a whole of parts, the EV draws consequences

---

[1] Cornford (224), indeed, takes 245b7 to mean 'if the real has the property of being in a sense one, it will evidently not be the same thing as
Unity'. But this is not a new proof depending on some such assumption
as Moravcsik suggests: it is rather a summary recapitulation of the
argument about the possession of parts (245a).

first on the hypothesis that 'Wholeness' exists, and then on the hypothesis that 'Wholeness' does not exist. He takes τὸ ὅλον to mean 'Wholeness' throughout except in the opening question (244d14), which seems somewhat arbitrary;[1] and he too fails adequately to explain why on the former hypothesis it should follow that the Real and Wholeness have separate natures. 'The Real', he says (225), 'since it does not even partake of Wholeness, will "fall short of itself" in the sense that it does not include Wholeness, which nevertheless is real.' But the premiss has simply been that 'what is' is 'not a whole', and it does not necessarily follow that it is not identical with or 'does not include' Wholeness—unless we are meant to assume that Wholeness itself must be a whole. Such an assumption might be based on 245d4–6, if the assertion there is taken as Moravcsik takes it; but that assertion has not yet been made. Alternatively, it might be based on the assumption that such things as Wholeness are 'self-predicational' and must themselves possess the qualities that they represent. But the words at 245c5, 'And so on this reasoning', which seem to introduce the consequence about 'separate natures' (c9) as well as the consequence about 'not being' (c6), suggest that there is some *argument*, which has *already* been presented, to justify the conclusions stated; and there has been no argument which would justify the conclusion that 'what is' is not Wholeness.

We may therefore reject the idea that τὸ ὅλον means Wholeness anywhere in this passage, and interpret thus. The 'one' or 'what is' of the monists is also called 'the whole', as though all *three* names, in fact, referred to a

[1] In 245d he prints 'wholeness' without the capital letter which he has hitherto given it.

single thing. But a 'whole' such as Parmenides describes, with extension in space, must have parts, and though it may, *qua* whole, have the character of 'the one', it cannot be the same as 'the one' of the monists, which is so called precisely because it is supposed to have no parts. Now, (1) do we say that 'what is' has unification of this sort and so is in a sense 'one' and therefore a 'whole', or (2) do we reject the idea that it is a 'whole'? If (1), then in view of its parts 'what is' cannot be identical with 'the one', and we have a plurality. If (2) we deny that 'what is' is a unified whole, but (i) still allow that there is a 'whole', then (a) since the former is incomplete and the latter presumably complete, the two must be distinct and 'what is' will 'not be' (i.e. it will not be 'the whole'),[1] while (b) we again have a plurality ('what is' and 'the whole'). If on the other hand, (ii) while denying that 'what is' is a unified whole we also say that 'the whole' does not exist, then the same must be true of 'what is'—it too cannot 'be', and indeed it could never have come to be; for anything that comes to be can only come to be as a whole, so that if we deny that there is a 'whole', there can be no 'being' either, and no coming-into-being. Furthermore, what is not a whole cannot even be of any definite number.

There is no difficulty in taking τὸ ὅλον in 245d5 to mean 'the whole' once we recognize that 'being' (οὐσία) here has special reference to the monists' 'what is'. The sentence as a whole is an explanation of the two statements contained in 245c11–d2. If the monists try to escape from their dilemma not only by withholding the

---

[1] Cf. appendix to this chapter. On almost any interpretation, 245c6 involves fallacious treatment of the identitative sense of 'to be', which it is one of the EV's aims to distinguish (for references see p. 66, n. 1). Presumably he is here allowing himself an *ad hominem* argument.

title of 'the whole' from their 'what is' but by denying the existence of a 'whole' altogether, they forfeit their right to talk about 'what is'; for if that *is*, it must be a whole.[1] This objection incidentally holds good even against hypothesis 2(i)—even, that is, if they take only the first step; but the EV has preferred to indicate some other difficulties that arise if they do that.

Of the two final points, those concerning coming-into-being and number, Cornford (227) remarks: 'These conclusions do not convict Parmenides of inconsistency, since he denied the possibility of coming-into-being and of plurality. They seem to be noted as the two most glaring deficiencies of his system.' This may possibly be the case. We have already seen that in the interests of common sense the possibility of applying names to 'what is' has been assumed.[2] It would not be unreasonable now to add in these two conclusions for the benefit of the 'common sense' reader, who denied neither genesis nor plurality. Nevertheless, if this is what is happening, it seems unnecessary and rather strange to present such conclusions as though they indicated inconsistencies, and it seems at least possible to explain each of them differently. (i) The objection that what is not a whole cannot be of any definite number may well be taken to mean that 'what is', if it is *ex hypothesi* not a whole, cannot even be described as 'one'. We have seen that repudiating 'the whole' means repudiating 'what is'. We now see that it also means repudiating 'the one'.[3] (ii) The remarks about

---

[1] [This stage of Plato's argument, unlike 244cd, is not valid against a thoroughgoing monism, because it confuses two different senses of 'whole'. At 245a it is stated to mean 'a whole of parts', whereas it is now used in the sense of 'entire'. While it is true that nothing can 'be' except as a whole, in this latter sense, it is not true that nothing can exist except as a whole of parts.]   [2] See p. 73, n. 1.

[3] This view is possible only if the words τὸ ἕν ἤ at 245d5 are excised,

coming-into-being cannot, indeed, be taken as revealing an inconsistency in Parmenides' doctrine, but it is not certain that the present argument against 'those who say that the All is one thing' (244b) is aimed at Parmenides or the Eleatics alone, though no doubt it is aimed primarily at them. It is equally capable of being applied to any monist whose *one thing* was (a) regarded (whether by himself, by Plato or by anyone else) as having no 'parts' but as constituting by itself *what is* and *the whole* (or 'the All'), (b) was spoken of in these three different ways, and (c) was treated as having extension in space. It seems possible that Plato may have had in mind the Milesian monists (who believed in 'coming-into-being') as well as the Eleatics, and that the present point is made with reference to their kind of monism.

3. CONCLUSION

In essaying the task of disproving Parmenides' dictum and showing that what is not in some sense is, and that what is in a way is not, the EV has begun by considering the nature of 'what is', and has first turned to such existing theories as maintained that there is a specific number of 'things that are', whether a plurality or only one. He has shown that pluralists and monists alike have been inconsistent. But two points also emerge from the discussion that will be of positive value. (i) Being is something separate from and additional to what pluralists have said 'is', and should be acknowledged as an independent entity in its own right. (ii) Although the

for otherwise the assumption is that 'the one' has already been repudiated along with 'the whole'. But as we have seen, those words almost certainly should be excised (p. 75, n. 2).

application to a Parmenidean 'one' of the 'names' 'what is', 'one', and 'the whole' involves contradictions, it would seem nevertheless that 'what is' must be 'one' and a 'whole' in a way—a hint, perhaps, that attribution must be distinguished from identification.

APPENDIX

The discussion of 244d–245d in the body of the chapter (section 2) concentrated on points of interpretation relevant to the main lines of the argument. But some points of detail in the passage, over which differences of opinion exist, must now be treated more fully. They are taken here in the order in which they occur in the text.

(a) *245a1–3*. Moravcsik (31 n. 3) thinks that nothing is said here about a whole of parts being itself a unity. The relevant Greek words are πάθος μὲν τοῦ ἑνὸς ἔχειν ἐπὶ τοῖς μέρεσι πᾶσιν οὐδὲν ἀποκωλύει. Moravcsik rejects Cornford's translation, which in essentials is the same as that given above, objecting that 'it is not the whole but only the parts that are said to be units'. He explains the passage thus (31): 'Having parts it is not prevented from being affected by the One in respect of its parts (i.e. each part is a unit). Thus the totality exists, it is a whole, and it is one.' Now in the first place, to obtain this sense Moravcsik would presumably have to translate πᾶν τε ὂν καὶ ὅλον as *'although* it is a sum and a whole', but the preceding ταύτῃ ('in this way') makes giving a concessive force to the participle very awkward. But it is clear in any case from 245b (and Moravcsik himself seems to allow it) that 'what is', although possessing parts, can itself be described as 'one', and it seems unlikely that Plato would have described anything as 'one' simply because it had parts that were units. The Greek can perfectly well mean that the aggregate is a unity (see p. 74, n. 3).

(b) *245c1–2*. 'Through having been affected by that character' (διὰ τὸ πεπονθέναι τὸ ὑπ' ἐκείνου πάθος) almost certainly means 'through having been affected by "the one" '. 'The one' was mentioned in the previous sentence; and it is difficult to see how ἐκείνου ('that character') could possibly refer to 'the whole'. Moravcsik (33, n. 1), however, insists that ἐκείνου must refer to 'Wholeness', arguing that 'an entity is not whole in virtue of its participation of the One, but in virtue of its participation of the Whole'. Here we may compare 245b, to which there is undoubtedly an allusion in the present sentence: 'Will "what is" have been affected by "the one" and in this way be "one" *and* "*whole*" . . . ?' It may be that being in some way a unity is regarded as essential to being a whole, and that all the EV means to say now is, 'If "what is" is not "one" *and therefore* not a whole. . . .' But it is also possible that it is assumed that if a thing is 'one', it *must* be a whole. As has been suggested above, the final sentence of the passage (245d8–10) may be taken to mean that what is not a whole cannot be 'one' (see p. 81, n. 3), from which it will follow that being 'one' entails being a whole; and it is possible that this idea is already implicit in the present sentence.

(c) *245c6*. Cornford (225) writes that the words οὐκ ὂν ἔσται τὸ ὄν 'may mean "the Real will be a thing that is not", i.e. a thing of which the negative statement is true, that it "is not" the same as Wholeness. Or they can be rendered . . .: "the Real will not be a thing that is" (for it is not the same as Wholeness, and Wholeness is a

thing that is). Both renderings amount to the same
thing.' He prefers the second, however, on the ground
that the words 'so on this line of argument also' (245c5)
suggest that the present conclusion is parallel to the conclusion at 245b8. Now we have seen above that the entity
which is held in 245c9 to be non-identical with 'what is'
cannot be Wholeness. In fact Cornford's interpretation
here becomes much more acceptable if we substitute for
'Wholeness' 'the whole' of the monists, and take this
'whole' to be the 'thing that is' with which 'what is' is
not identical. Such a conclusion would be justified by the
remarks about 'what is' 'falling short of itself' and 'being
deprived of itself'. But οὐκ ὂν ἔσται τὸ ὄν is very odd
Greek for 'will not be a thing that is', if this is supposed
to mean that it will not be (identical with) some (other)
thing to which we attribute being. It may be added that
Cornford's insertion of 'also' after 'on this reasoning' is
not necessitated by the Greek, so that it is unnecessary to
look for a conclusion parallel to that of 245b8.

There is something to be said for Taylor's translation,
'being *will not be being*,' which he supports by remarking
(141 n.) that 'there will be being which is not included
in being; there is a formal incompatibility between . . . (1)
being is not a whole, (2) there *is* a totality of being'.
Indeed, the only objection to this is that one would
expect the article, were this the EV's meaning—οὐ τὸ ὂν
ἔσται τὸ ὄν.

But there is another possible interpretation, which on
the whole it seems best to adopt. We may take οὐκ ὂν
ἔσται τὸ ὄν to mean that 'what is' (as being 'deprived of
itself' and 'falling short of itself') will have the attribute
of 'not being' (something). Whereas the monists apply
to what they regard as real the epithet or 'name' of ὄν

('being'), they must now recognize that if it is not itself a whole but there is nevertheless a 'whole', it will itself be incomplete and so deserves to be described as οὐκ ὄν ('not being'); for it *is not* (identical with) (i) that (whatever it may be) by which it falls short of completeness, or (ii) 'the whole' (see p. 80 n.). Whether it is (i) or (ii) that the EV has in mind hardly matters.

(d) *245c9*. However one may wish to interpret 245c6, one might imagine that something incomplete could hardly be supposed to have a 'nature' of its own. But the leading premiss, that 'what is' is not a whole, is itself absurd. If 'what is' *is* incomplete, it must be distinct from what is (*ex hypothesi*) 'the whole'.

(e) *245c11–d1*. According to Cornford (226), the words ταὐτὰ ταῦτα ('this same conclusion' or 'these same conclusions') refer to the consequences mentioned in 245c6–8, and mean that if there is no such thing as 'Wholeness' (as he interprets τὸ ὅλον), no less than if there is, '(1) the Real will not be a thing that is, and (2) all things will be a plurality'. But he finds it difficult to understand how these consequences, which followed from the premisses that 'what is' is not whole and that 'Wholeness' exists, can still be supposed to follow now that 'Wholeness' is (*ex hypothesi*) *not* a thing that is. He therefore has recourse to a very difficult and unlikely solution:

The present supposition is: that the Real has not the unity belonging to a whole, and there is no such thing as Wholeness. It follows that the Real, having no unity or wholeness (for there is no such thing), must be a plurality without any unity. This gives the second consequence 'all things will be more than one'—not two this time, but an unlimited plurality (ἄπειρα). The first consequence 'the Real will not be a thing that is (ὄν)' is actually repeated here in the words 'besides not being a thing that is' (πρὸς τῷ μὴ εἶναι . . . ὄν). This cannot now mean that the Real is not the same as Wholeness (a thing that is); for we are now supposing that Wholeness is *not* 'a thing that is'. But there is a sense in which the words (οὐκ ὂν ἔσται τὸ ὄν) will be true. The Real will not be *a* thing that is (ὄν in the singular), because the Real is now an indefinite plurality without any unity.

Cornford admits that his solution may seem far-fetched, but reminds us of the *Parmenides*, 'where similar arguments are set out at length'. It is certainly difficult to believe that we have an allusion to a consequence (the Real will not be a thing that is, viz. Wholeness) which now has to be interpreted with special emphasis on the singularity of the participle (the Real will not be *a* thing that is). It is also rather difficult to believe that we are meant to deduce, having read the *Parmenides*, that because 'what is' is not a whole and does not possess the unity proper to a whole, it must be an unlimited plurality. Such a solution should only be adopted as a last resort.

It is far easier and more natural to suppose that ταὐτὰ ταῦτα alludes, not to the results enunciated (in 245c6–9) of the hypothesis that 'what is' is not a whole although 'the whole' exists, but simply to the non-existence which has just been attributed to 'the whole' as a new hypothesis. If 'the whole' does not exist, then neither does 'what is'—because, as the EV goes on to explain, 'what is', in order to 'be' at all, would *have* to be a whole (and therefore 'the whole').

It is another disadvantage of Cornford's view that he has to attach the ὄν at the end of the sentence to πρὸς τῷ μὴ εἶναι ('in addition to not being') in order to find his 'first consequence' repeated here. On the present view, these words without the ὄν contain the whole of what is meant by ταὐτὰ ταῦτα, which expression, though plural in form, is quite capable of referring to a single statement.

CHAPTER IV: 245e–249d

VIEWS ABOUT 'WHAT IS'—
MATERIALISTS AND IDEALISTS

I. MATERIALISTS

The EV now passes from 'those who give an exact account of "what is" and "what is not" ' to 'those who put the matter in a different way' (245e); that is to say, from 'those who set out to determine precisely the number as well as the nature of the things that are' (242c), to those who assert either that true reality consists solely of 'certain intelligible and bodiless Forms' (246b) or that that alone is real which can be touched and handled (which they equate with body) (246a–b). The quarrel between these two latter groups is likened to a Battle of Gods and Giants.

There can be little doubt that, as Cornford (232) says, 'the Giants include all—philosophers or average men— who believe that tangible body is the sole reality', and that Plato is discussing 'the tendency of thought that he defines, not one or another set of individuals who, more or less, exhibited that tendency'. Strictly interpreted, however, the contrast in 245e should imply that the Presocratics who have already been discussed are not, as Cornford (228 f., 231) supposes they are, included among the materialists now under consideration. These materialists, whom Theaetetus agrees must be considered 'also' (246a3), seem to be people who have *not* tried precisely to enumerate 'the things that are'. Indeed the only real argument against taking the view that from now on we are concerned with different people altogether is that there appears to be an allusion to Parmenides at 249c–d:

'the philosopher must not accept the theory that the All
is at rest, either from those who talk about "one" or
those who talk about the many Forms'. This allusion,
however, may have been inserted quite incidentally, for
the only idealists the EV has in mind when he is talking
about the Battle (246b), or again when he considers the
idealists in particular (248a), appear to be the 'Friends of
Forms'.

So far as the materialists are concerned, the remark that
the true Giants would accept as real only what can be
'squeezed' (247c), and the tone of mild ridicule with which
they are treated throughout, suggest perhaps that Plato
is thinking primarily of some of his own contemporaries,
and in particular of some who may have consciously and
deliberately opposed his own philosophy. 'This battle
of Gods and Giants', says Cornford (232), 'is a philosophic battle, not a battle of one school of idealists
against the unthinking average man.' But it is not impossible that Plato is thinking primarily of 'average men',
and that it is he himself who turns the battle into a
'philosophic' one.

There seem at any rate to be insufficient grounds for
supposing that the monists and pluralists 'appear as the
ancestors of the two parties in the Battle of Gods and
Giants', or that the question put earlier to the Ionian
physicists, 'What do you mean by real?' receives 'the
beginnings of an answer' in what is said about the
materialists' description of it as tangible body, and a
final answer in the mark of reality suggested by the EV
presently, 'the power of acting and being acted upon'
(Cornford, 218, 231, 238). The pluralists are not necessarily only physical philosophers,[1] and the Milesians may

[1] See p. 69.

be included among the monists.[1] The evidence, such as it is, suggests that there is no such connection as Cornford finds between the two groups. If Plato was thinking of any earlier philosophers in discussing the Giants, they may well be the Atomists, who assigned no definite number to 'the things that are'.[2]

The EV says that he will ask each of the two parties, Giants and Gods, for an account or explanation (λόγον) of the being (οὐσία) which it posits (246c). He considers first the materialists, and for the sake of the argument imagines 'those whose violence would drag everything down to the level of body' to be sufficiently 'reformed' to answer questions in a civil manner (246d). They will agree that there is such a thing as a mortal living creature, i.e. a body animated by a soul, thus giving to soul a place among 'the things that are' (246e). They will further agree that one soul may be just, another unjust, through the presence in it of justice or injustice, and also that 'justice, wisdom and all the other virtues and their opposites', as being capable of being present or absent, must exist (247a f.), although they are invisible.[3]

[1] See p. 82.

[2] Cornford (232, n. 1) is probably right in holding that their recognition of void would not exclude them. Moravcsik (35, n. 1) holds that the argument is against empiricists, and Democritus was a materialist but not an empiricist. But the people concerned 'define reality as body' (246b1), and allow that soul exists, claiming that it is body (246e, 247b). These are their own assertions. Plato is not, as Moravcsik claims he is (36, n. 2), ' "improving" the empiricist position in ascribing to it the postulation of the soul', nor is it simply 'for the sake of the argument' that they hold the view that it is material. The point in which their 'reform' consists is the admission that some immaterial things are real, e.g. justice and wisdom (247b–d). They are not out-and-out empiricists, but they are (unless reformed) out-and-out materialists.

[3] Cornford (238) says that the materialists are 'brought some of the way towards the full admission that not merely the justice residing in an individual soul, but Justice itself, is real'. But since the mark of being able to affect or be affected is intended to apply to such bodiless things

Will they also say that these things have body? Theaetetus replies that the soul, they believe, possesses a sort of body, but so far as wisdom and other such qualities are concerned, they hardly dare to assert that they are simply nothing, *or* that they are all bodies. That shows, says the EV, that they are genuinely reformed characters, for the true 'seed of the dragon' would insist that what is intangible is just nothing at all (247c). Now, what do they refer to when they say that both kinds of thing 'are'— what is it that inheres both in bodiless things and in the things that have body, which enables them to say that (247d)? If they cannot answer, would they admit that 'what is' is like this?

I say that anything really is which possesses any sort of potentiality either to affect something in any way, or to be affected—even to the slightest extent by the most trivial agent, and even though it be only once. I am proposing as a mark to distinguish the 'things that are', that they are simply *power*.[1]

In the EV's opinion, it seems, and probably in Plato's, out-and-out materialists would never make any concessions to those who believed in bodiless things, and it would be most unlikely that a true reformation of such materialists could ever be achieved (246d, 247c). The reform is only *imagined* for the sake of the argument, which is addressed rather to the 'common-sense' reader

(see below), the materialists in accepting the mark are in fact virtually accepting the Form.

[1] As Cornford says (234, n. 1), we might expect the EV to be saying in this last sentence that the *mark*, not the 'things that are' themselves, is simply power. Possibly we should read δύναμιν. But a 'power' (δύναμις) is the property which reveals in its action the nature of a thing (cf. Souilhé, 154 ff.), and as being peculiar to a particular thing (at least so far as Forms are concerned), might easily be identified with the thing itself. The 'being' of a thing is simply the function that it performs.

than to the materialists themselves. Only if it is acknowledged that justice and wisdom and the like are real will
there be any common ground on which the discussion
can proceed.

The EV is no longer concerned with insisting that
Being (the concept) is something other than what has
been posited as real. The materialists, who are supposed
to allow that some bodiless things are real, do not specify
that there is only some particular number of real things,
and the question now is of a different kind. What is
wanted is an explanation (λόγος) of what they regard as
real, an account of what is involved in being real.[1] The
EV's own suggestion, 'a power to affect something or to
be affected', is one that the 'reformed' materialists might
reasonably be expected to accept; and, as we shall see,
it is one that reasonable idealists ought to accept as well.
But in making this suggestion the EV is offering only a
mark (ὅρος) of what is real, not a definition (λόγος) of the
'essence' of Being.[1]

2. IDEALISTS

Theaetetus having accepted the distinguishing mark on
behalf of the materialists, the EV now offers it to the

[1] Moravcsik (35 f.) remarks that Plato 'does not question the claim that
the empirically given exists. This contrasts with the claims of the *Republic*
and the *Timaeus* . . . Plato demands of the empiricists only that they admit
the existence of something immaterial. "This will suffice" he says (247c9-
d1). The admission will not suffice to support the ontology of the middle
dialogues.' But Plato never denied that phenomena have a degree of
being, and not infrequently uses εἶναι ('to be') of them. Cf. Cherniss,
AJP 78 (1957), 239 ff. We need not expect Plato to distinguish between
degrees of being where such a distinction is irrelevant.

[2] [Owen (229, n. 14), arguing against the view of Moravcsik (28) that
Plato is concerned to show that existence is indefinable, would give ὅρος
here the unqualified sense of 'definition' which it possesses in many other
passages.]

idealists. It seems clear, though the question has been much debated, that the idealists' theory represents Plato's own theory of Forms, as propounded in the *Phaedo* and the *Republic*, which he now wishes to modify.[1] The views attributed to the idealists are in full accord with what had been Plato's theory, but in important respects do not fit Parmenides or the Pythagoreans; nor do we know of anyone else who held such views. The idealists are said to regard what the materialists treat as 'being' as simply 'a sort of moving process of becoming' (246c), and to maintain that we have intercourse with it through the senses, whereas with true being, which is constant, never changing (ἀεὶ κατὰ ταὐτὰ ὡσαύτως ἔχειν), we have intercourse only through thought by means of the soul (248a).

What, asks the EV, do the idealists really mean by this 'intercourse'? Must it not be precisely what has just been described, 'an affecting or being affected that arises from the things that encounter one another through some power' (248b)? But the idealists, says the EV, will maintain that while 'becoming' has the power to affect or be affected, neither of these things is appropriate to 'being' (248c). Nevertheless a soul is capable of knowing, and 'being' of being known. What, then, about knowing and being known—is either or both of these an affecting or being affected, or does neither of them come under either head? 'Evidently neither comes under either head', says Theaetetus. 'Otherwise our friends would be contradicting what they said earlier' (248d). The allusion

[1] Cf. Cornford (242 ff.), who discusses other views. That Plato should here be modifying either the presentation or the substance of his theory accords with the *Parmenides*: cf. Bluck, *CQ* 6 (1956), 29.
[See Crombie (Vol. II, p. 419 ff.) for further arguments against the view that Plato is modifying the substance of the theory of Forms. Cf. Kamlah, 35 ff.]

here, as is plain from the EV's next remark, is to 248a,
where the view was attributed to the idealists that 'being'
is constant and unchanging; the idealists' assumed reluc-
tance to accept the EV's proposed distinguishing mark
as appropriate to 'being' is due to its apparent implication
that 'being' can undergo change of some kind.

To this declaration by Theaetetus that the idealists
would be contradicting their earlier assertion if they admitted that knowing or being known involved affecting
or being affected, the EV replies (248d–e):

I see what you mean. They would have to say this: If knowing is to be acting on something, it follows that what is known
must be acted upon by it; and so, on this showing, Reality
when it is being known by the act of knowledge must, in so
far as it is known, be changed owing to being so acted upon;
and that, we say, cannot happen to the changeless.

This is Cornford's rendering, and probably correct. At
the beginning he reads μανθάνω· τόδε γε and understands
λέγοιεν ἄν from the previous sentence.[1] 'What follows',
he writes (240, n. 3), 'is put into the mouths of the
Idealists, who state their objection to regarding knowing
as an action. They are allowed to ignore the possibility
that knowing is an affection of the soul, acted upon by
the object. M. Diès prints τόδε γε, but translates τὸ δέ or
τὸ δέ γε: "mais ceci, au moins, ils l'avoueront"—a
rendering which makes the Stranger force on the Idealists
the alternative that knowing is an action.'

The EV continues, again in Cornford's translation
(248e–249b):

---

[1] It is tempting (cf. Taylor, 147 n.) to omit the colon after μανθάνω and
translate, 'I know this much at any rate, that if knowing is to be acting

But tell me, in heaven's name: are we really to be so easily convinced that change, life, soul, understanding have no place in that which is perfectly real—that it has neither life nor thought, but stands immutable in solemn aloofness, devoid of intelligence? . . . But can we say it has intelligence without having life? . . . But if we say it contains both, can we deny that it has soul in which they reside? . . . But then, if it has intelligence, life, and soul, can we say that a living thing remains at rest in complete changelessness? . . . In that case we must admit that what changes and change itself are real things.

Whereas in the *Phaedo* and *Republic* Plato excludes change from what is real, he here acknowledges that since souls must belong to 'what is', and souls undergo change, 'change' and 'that which changes' must belong to 'what is'. Moravcsik (38) thinks that Plato is here 'showing that the sharp dichotomy between "being" and "becoming" is untenable'. But even if 'that which changes' (τὸ κινούμενον) had to be taken to include the whole realm of 'becoming', 'what is' might be taken to include whatever has any degree of being; the expression and its cognates are used in that sense elsewhere. There is therefore no need in any case to suppose that 'becoming' has been up-graded to the rank of 'being'. But apart from the fact that to introduce here the degrees-of-reality theory would contribute nothing to the main discussion, there has been nothing in the argument to warrant any conclusion about 'becoming'. In its context, therefore, 'that which changes' probably means no more than 'that which undergoes such change as soul, life and intelligence involve' (cf. Cherniss, *Aristotle's Criticism*, vol. 1, 437 ff.;

on something', etc. But the 'we say' at the end is a little awkward on this view.

AJP 78 (1957), 238 f.). In that case, *if* the objects of knowledge are not changed by being known, the expression presumably covers nothing but souls (as presumably on Ross' view, 110 f.).

But Cornford himself remarks (245) that as the EV's present outburst follows immediately upon the idealist's objection that reality cannot be affected by being known because then it would be changed, 'it appears at first sight as if the Stranger himself must think that what is known is changed by being known'. Although Cornford rejects this implication, on the grounds that the argument later (249c) 'excludes the idea that the nature or content of a Form could possibly be altered by the act of knowledge', and prefers to accept (247) that 'the question whether knowing and being known do not involve something analogous to the physical intercourse of perception seems to be left unanswered', it is doubtful whether he is right to do so. Another interpretation of the problem is possible, by which knowledge may be allowed to involve some change in its objects without infringing the sanctity of the actual nature of Forms.

It is clear from the argument against the monists (245a) that the expression 'to be affected by' need mean no more than 'to possess the quality of'. A whole is 'affected by "the one" ' inasmuch as it is unified; if the materialists who are represented as accepting the distinguishing mark were asked how it applied to justice or wisdom, which they admit to 'be', they would presumably cite the fact that a soul can *be just* or *be wise*. (For the meaning of the expression cf. further *Parmenides* 160a6–7, 164b5–6; see Moravcsik, 37.) Whatever may be the case with a soul that 'is affected', the 'affecting' concerned need not be supposed to change the *nature* of justice or wisdom. Now

if any of the 'unchanging' things that the idealists regard
as having being is known, it might be said that 'known'
can be predicated of it, that it has the quality of being
known, and so 'is affected'; but there will be no need to
suppose that the *nature* of the thing affected is thereby
changed. The thing will be 'changed', but only inasmuch
as it has acquired an inessential attribute. (Cf. Moravcsik
40: 'The Forms are subject to change and motion only
in the sense that dated (temporal) propositions are true
of them.')

This interpretation allows us to follow the natural
logic of the argument, and understand the EV to be
offering an affirmative answer, in contradiction to the
idealists, to the question whether knowing is an action
or affecting. Even if it were a being-acted-upon or a
being-affected, the object known could still be regarded
as 'changed', to the very limited extent required by the
argument, by virtue of the fact that it acquires the
attribute of 'being known'. Perhaps both knowing and
being known should come under the heading of both
affecting and being affected, just as in the *Theaetetus*,
where the process of sense-perception is described (156a–
157a), eye and object alike are both active and passive.
So long as we distinguish between change of attribute
and change of nature, no difficulty is involved in such an
admission.

If therefore, as seems probable, the objects of knowledge are regarded as 'changing' in respect of what may
be attributed to them, the expression 'that which changes'
will also cover Forms in respect of their being known.
At first sight this conclusion may not seem plausible.
But if we are *not* meant to take it that being known incurs
change, then apart from (i) the fact that Forms certainly

acquire the attribute of 'being known', which would appear to count as 'being affected', and (ii) the difficulty of explaining why the question whether knowing implies affecting should be raised and left unanswered, there is (iii) the problem why the distinguishing mark of reality should *not* have been applied to the Forms, and (iv) the difficulty that the discussion of this mark, if it is not meant to suggest that Forms 'are affected', would seem to have little or no bearing on the main argument of the dialogue. If, on the other hand, being known *is* supposed to involve change, then the point that Forms can undergo change *in this way*—in respect of inessential attributes, though not in respect of their natures—is of supreme importance for the main argument. This distinction is an aspect of the distinction between identity and attribution, which it is one of the EV's chief aims to elucidate.[1]

The EV continues (249b–d):

The result is that (a) if all things are changeless, intelligence cannot exist in anything anywhere with regard to any object. . . . And yet (b) if we allow that everything is being moved and changed, on this view also we shall be excluding this same thing from the number of 'the things that are'. . . . Do you think that without rest (στάσις) there could ever be constancy of relationships, condition and orientation (τὸ κατὰ ταὐτὰ καὶ ὡσαύτως καὶ περὶ τὸ αὐτό)? . . . Well, without that do you see intelligence existing or capable of existing anywhere? . . . Yet we must fight with all the force of reason against anyone who allows knowledge or understanding or intelligence not to exist, and yet makes assertions about something, whatever it may be. . . . The man who is a philosopher and has a high respect for these qualities must necessarily, it seems, refuse to accept from those who talk about 'one' thing or the many Forms that the All is static, while at

[1] For references, see p. 66, n. 1.

the same time he must not for a moment listen to those who make 'what is' change in every respect. Like a child begging for 'both', he must say that 'what is' and the All consists of what is changeless *and* what is in change—both together.

The final sentence of this extract is puzzling, and is the only sentence here which might cast doubt on the view that being known is supposed to imply 'change' in the object. If 'what is in change' does include Forms (inasmuch as they come to be known), it might seem odd to couple this phrase, apparently in contrast, with 'what is changeless', which certainly refers to the nature of Forms. The language would imply a contrast between two different classes of objects, when what is needed is a contrast between different respects in which the same objects can or cannot be changed. Even on Moravcsik's view, the things concerned are 'in one sense in motion, and in another sense at rest' (38). It is not a question of two different classes of things.

However, the exact form of expression may be due to the comparison with the child begging.[1] In any case some looseness of language is inevitable, since the essential distinction between identity and attribution, on which the present 'paradox' concerning changelessness and changeability in the Forms rests, has yet to be explained fully. It remains for the moment a matter of some puzzlement. There is not sufficient evidence here, therefore, for the rejection of the view that being known implies change.[2]

[1] It is usually supposed that the allusion is to a child's desire, when faced with a choice, to have 'both'. But Taylor (149) could be right when he says 'to wish for "things unmoving or moving" seems to be a formula for wishing for "everything and anything" '.

[2] [Although Bluck gives considerable prominence to the idea that knowledge is here presented as involving 'change' in its objects, and

The natures of the Forms do not change. If they did,
there could be no constancy, which is necessary to intelligence and therefore to the making of any assertion.
The language used about constancy is very similar to that
used at 248a of the idealists' conception of 'being', and
indeed so far as the natures of the Forms are concerned,
they are right. But as the materialists conceded that some
immaterial things are real, and accepted the EV's distinguishing mark of reality, so the idealists must give up
the idea that all things that really 'are' are absolutely and
without exception changeless, and (it is implied) themselves accept the mark.

3. CONCLUSION

The EV has turned from those who enumerate or name
what 'is' to those who give some sort of account of the
nature of what is. He himself suggests a distinguishing
mark of it, a mark which requires that the existence of
some immaterial objects be acknowledged, and that
change should not be excluded from 'what is'. He has
also perhaps implied that objects of knowledge are capable of being 'affected' to the extent of acquiring or losing
inessential attributes, though not in respect of their
essential natures.[1] But although it is suggested that any

presents strong arguments to support his interpretation, he added at this
point the proviso that 'at the same time it cannot be considered in-
disputably correct'. This was not, I think, because he doubted its validity,
but reflects the fact that Plato does not spell the point out as clearly as he
might, and also that the case against the idealists is adequately made if
souls are subject to change and does not require Forms to be so too.]
    [1] [Bigger's far-reaching exposition (125 ff.) of the distinguishing mark
as an 'Ontological Principle' requiring that 'the primary form of any
metaphysical analysis must be relational' is probably intended to be
judged in the wider context of general Platonic interpretation; it certainly
goes well beyond what the text of the *Sophist* warrants.]

sensible person must reject both out-and-out materialism and the extreme view that anything that changes in any way cannot count as a thing that 'is', the nature of 'what is', as the EV goes on to show, requires further explanation. The crux, as we shall see, is the distinction between the 'proper nature' of a thing and what may be attributed to it, where the 'thing' concerned is what Plato would call a Form.[1]

[1] With pp. 99, 101 above cf. pp. 105f., 142, 151.

THE PUZZLE OF PREDICATION

I. THE NATURE OF BEING

The EV declares that the inquiry concerning 'what is' is still as baffling as ever, for in spite of the conclusion just reached, that it consists of what is changeless and of what changes, they might still be confronted with the very question that they put earlier on to the pluralists who declared that the All 'is' Hot and Cold. This question, it will be remembered, was what is meant by 'is'; and although it was established that Being could not be identified with either or with both, the question *what* it is—what 'to be' *means*—was raised but never answered. To declare that the All 'is' what is changeless and what is in change is merely to take up a position similar to that of the dualists and to be faced with the same question.

The EV now argues again, on lines similar to those on which he argued before, that Being is an entity in its own right, separate from all others. He does not repeat the question asked at 243d–e, but says that he will remind Theaetetus what it was by questioning him 'in the same way' as he questioned the pluralists. The argument that follows is based on simple substitution (250a–b).

Well, don't you say that Change and Rest are complete opposites? . . . Yet you say equally of each of them and of both that they *are*? . . . When you allow that they *are*, do you mean that they both (and each severally) change? . . . Or are you indicating that they are both at a standstill? . . . So when you said they both are, you were counting Being as a third thing over and above these two, and taking Rest and

Change as embraced by it, and having regard to their communion with Being?

Theaetetus replies, 'Yes, it seems as though we really
do have an intuition of Being as a third thing, when we
say that Change and Rest are'; and the EV adds, 'So
Being is not Change and Rest, both together, but something different from them'. This is no doubt meant to
recall the conclusion at 249d that ' "what is" and the All
consists of what is changeless and of what is in change—
both together'. The Greek for 'what is' and for Being is
the same (τὸ ὄν), and it may be, as Cornford (250) thinks,
that the present remark 'appears to Theaetetus to be a
contradiction' of 249d. But there is nothing in any of
Theaetetus' replies to suggest that this is so, and the
reference to the question put to the pluralists, combined
with the argument at 250a–b, should have made it clear
that we are concerned with the meaning of 'are', the
concept of Being; and the EV is now talking about
Change and Rest, not about changing and changeless
things. Despite the inevitable ambiguity of τὸ ὄν, there
is no good reason to suppose, as Peck does (*CQ* 1952,
43), that this ambiguity is causing trouble here.

The point of the allusion to 249d is much more likely
to be, quite simply, that since 'what is' consists of what is
changeless and of what is in change, we might have
expected to be able to identify the concept of Being with
'Rest plus Change'. It will be recalled that in the argument against the pluralists the possibility was considered
of identifying Being with the Hot and the Cold combined
as well as with each separately.[1] No argument is offered
to prove that Being is not Change *and* Rest, probably

[1] See p. 70f.

because Theaetetus has already admitted that it seems to be a third thing.

The EV's next remark does, however, cause perplexity: 'In virtue of its own nature, then, Being is neither at a standstill nor changing' (250c6). This is taken to follow from the fact that Being is not identical with either Rest or Change or both together. Runciman (94) calls this an 'erroneous deduction' which must be interpreted 'as Plato's conscious statement of an unreal difficulty which . . . is duly to be resolved'. But the point is that neither being at rest nor being in change is included within the meaning (or 'nature') of Being. It is puzzling for Theaetetus because, as the EV says (250c–d), 'If a thing is not changing, how can it not be at a standstill? Or how can what is in no way at a standstill not be changing?' This shows that the puzzlement is due to difficulty in distinguishing between the 'proper nature' of a thing and its attributes—a difficulty which the EV will go to considerable lengths, for the sake of his main argument, to resolve.[1]

The EV observes that whereas they were previously perplexed about the question to what the name 'what is not' should be applied, they are now no less puzzled about 'what is' (250d–e).[2] The reason for this will be that,

---

[1] 'The reader', says Cornford (248 f.), 'who, like Theaetetus, does not see that "Reality" has ceased to mean "the real" and now means "realness" will agree to the Stranger's concluding remark that Reality is as puzzling as unreality.' But τὸ ὄν in the EV's conclusion at 250e6 probably means 'what is' (see n. 2 below); and in what follows he offers an explanation not of the difference between 'what is' and Being, but only of the difference between 'proper natures' and attributes.

[2] Although τὸ ὄν has recently been used to mean Being, there is no difficulty about the transition here to the meaning 'what is', particularly in view of the allusion to τὸ μὴ ὄν. The central problem is better understood as concerned with 'what is' and 'what is not' than with Being and Not-being. This seems to be confirmed by 245e, where the same problem was mentioned; there the two expressions were certainly used in the

quite apart from the difficulty of imagining anything that is neither at rest nor changing, Being (which is now counted as a 'thing that is') seems not to conform to what was said about 'what is'. It is the conclusion that this particular thing is (of its own nature) neither at rest nor changing that seems to contradict the conclusion at 249d3–4.

Finally, the EV says (250e–251a) that since 'what is' and 'what is not' are equally puzzling, there is hope that any light thrown upon the one will illuminate the other. This suggests that the solution will be similar in both cases. In what follows, light is in fact shed on 'what is', inasmuch as it is shown that a 'thing that is' (i) has a distinct nature of its own, but (ii) *participates* in Being and in other things (including Change and Rest). This not only resolves the problems of the present section, but does indeed illuminate the nature of 'what is not', for we find that a 'thing which is not' may be a thing that (i) has a distinct nature of its own, but (ii) participates in Otherness (as well as in other things). In both cases what is needed is an understanding of 'participation', that is to say, of attribution; and the elucidation of this requires an explanation of the difference between identification and predication.

2. ATTRIBUTION: THE COMMUNION OF KINDS

That an understanding of the nature of predication is what is needed, in the EV's view, for the explication of the problem of the thing that neither rests nor changes, and of 'what is' in general, is indicated when he proceeds to

sense 'what is' and 'what is not' in the first half of the sentence, and it would be unnatural to take them otherwise in the second half.

recall the puzzle of one man with many 'names' or attributes. 'We attribute to him colours and shapes and sizes. . . . Anyone can take a hand in the game and at once object that many things cannot be one, nor one thing many' (251a–b). But it is indicated even more clearly in what follows. For the puzzle of one man (or physical object) with many names is merely 'entertainment for the young and the late-learners' (251b). The important point is that things like Rest and Change (presently called 'Kinds') can also have several attributes, and this is the point that he goes on to demonstrate.

Having declared that the argument is to be addressed to 'all who have at any time discussed being (οὐσία) at all', he asks (251d),

Are we to refrain from attaching (προσάπτειν) Being (οὐσία) to Change and Rest or anything else to anything else, but to treat them in our discussions as incapable of mixing (ἄμεικτα) and unable to participate (μεταλαμβάνειν) in one another? Or are we to lump them all together as capable of associating (ἐπικοινωνεῖν) with one another? Or say that some can, some cannot?[1]

It would seem natural to assume that these various terms all refer to predication, since predication was the issue where the 'one man with many names' was concerned; and so they probably do. At the same time, they are all metaphors, and it would be very unsafe to assume that in the arguments to come they have a precise, technical meaning. Although they may be used in reference or allusion to what we would call predication, it does not follow that their *meaning* is necessarily bound up with the notion of predication. It may be remarked, however,

[1] The Greek terms in this quotation will be rendered consistently in what follows by the same English equivalents as are used here. Hence there will be no need to repeat the Greek words on every occasion.

that the other important term, 'communion' (κοινωνία), which the EV uses in 251e, was used at 250b9 very obviously with reference to what we should call attribution,[1] and is so used again here.

The EV supposes for the sake of argument that nothing has any capacity for communion with anything else. Then Change and Rest will not partake of (μετέχειν) Being. From this it would follow (252a) that Change and Rest would not *be*, if they had no share in (προσκοινωνεῖν) Being. But such a conclusion would make nonsense of the theories of those who claim that the All is changing, those who make it a static 'one', and those who say that the 'things that are' are to be found in constant and unchanging Forms. The point is that none of these assertions could be true if there were no such things as Change and Rest; and in fact, as the EV says, 'all these people attach (προσάπτειν) Being (τὸ εἶναι) either to Change or to Rest,[2] the one group saying that things *really* change (ὄντως κινεῖσθαι), the other that they are *really* at a standstill (ὄντως ἑστηκότ' εἶναι)'.[3] The 'attaching' here consists of putting an adverb ('really') with the verb, an indication that 'to attach' must not be interpreted too precisely; but the resulting statements, if true, entail the possibility of predicating Being of

[1] See p. 104. For a refutation of Cornford's denial (256 f.) that these terms refer to predication at all, see Ackrill (2 ff.) [Cornford has recently been defended by Sayre, 192 ff.].

[2] Cornford translates, 'they all attribute existence to things, some saying they really *are* in movement', etc. But this does not fit the context, which requires here a reason why the existence of Rest and Change is so crucial to all the theories under review. The translation given in the text makes the necessary point, that the theories all presuppose the existence of one or the other of these two concepts.

[3] The use of the plural ἑστηκότ' suggests that the EV is thinking of the Friends of Forms, but now leaving out the champions of 'the one'. For Plato it is the importance of communion to his own theory that matters most.

Change and Rest, since only if Change and Rest are is it
possible for anything ('really') to change or rest.

Likewise, if there were no 'mixing together' (σύμμειξις)
—and hence no such thing as Change—those cosmo-
logists who talk about things being separated out of and
combined into a unity or a set of elements would be
talking meaninglessly (λέγοιεν ἂν οὐδέν). 'Moreover
those who do not allow us to say that a thing has communion with a quality other than itself and to call it that
other thing would be carrying on their argument in the
most ludicrous way of all' (252b), because in stating their
theory they cannot avoid using expressions such as 'is',
'apart', 'from the rest' and 'by itself', and so by implication contradicting themselves. They imply that the
things they are talking about have communion with
Being, Otherness, and so on. Here again it seems clear
that communion implies the possession of an attribute.

It is also clearly suggested in this passage that if there
is no communion, there can be no statement-making at
all. Indeed if nothing has communion with Being, nothing
(if the argument is taken to its logical conclusion) will
exist. The EV does not take the argument as far as that.
But at least it seems likely that in associating those who
will not allow one man to be called by many names with
those who reject communion he is thinking throughout
of his opponents, not as people who allowed only
statements of identity (Ross, 112; Hamlyn, 295), or predication of a particular kind (Cornford, 254), but as
people who rejected any kind of attribution or predication and embraced what Moravcsik (59) calls 'a
thoroughgoing semantic atomism'. Probably they will
not have themselves recognized the absurdity of even
stating such a theory. But the passage as a whole suggests

that when they 'refuse to allow us to call a man good,
but only the good good, and the man man', they are
ruling out statements altogether, and that what they allow
is not the making of some particular kind of statement,
but only naming.[1]

At the same time we need not, with Moravcsik (57 f.),
deny that in mentioning the 'one man with many names'
Plato is alluding to 'the old question of how can one
particular partake of several Forms'. Moravcsik denies
this on the ground that 'this question is treated satisfactorily in *Parmenides* 129 ff'. But there is an allusion to it
again in the *Philebus* (14c ff.); and although the present
statement of the puzzle is indeed itself 'an example of
what is considered problematic by the opposing "sophists"', and all that they need to be shown at the
moment is that *anything* can have attributed to it 'things'
which are not identical with or essential to its own
nature, yet Plato may well have in mind also readers with
a knowledge of Platonic doctrine. To them, as to him,
there would be an important difference between the
question whether a physical object can have attributes
and the question whether a 'Kind' can, as is indicated in
the *Parmenides* passage itself. He might well, from the
dramatic point of view, treat 'the problem at issue here'
as 'naming versus stating in general', while *simultaneously*
intending to remind the initiated of the old question of
one particular partaking of several Forms, and so to
indicate that he is passing from that to the important
question of the attributes of Forms. This would give

[1] [Frede's attempt (62) to refute Moravcsik on this point is not very
convincing. The fact remains that if the 'late learners' had allowed statements of the type 'That is a man', it would have been open for Plato
(and surely irresistibly so) to criticize the inconsistency of their use of 'is'
in all such sentences, not just in the statement of their theory.]

point to the remark that the old question is simply 'entertainment for the young'.

Having dismissed the notion that nothing has the power of communion with anything else, the EV suggests that all things are capable of associating with (ἐπικοινωνία) one another. Theaetetus himself claims to be able to refute this suggestion. 'Change itself', he says, 'would come completely to a standstill (παντάπασιν ἵσταιτ' ἄν) and Rest itself would change, if each were to supervene upon the other (εἴπερ ἐπιγιγνοίσθην ἐπ' ἀλλήλοιν)' (252d6–8). 'But that, I suppose', asks the EV, 'is absolutely and necessarily impossible, that Change should come to a standstill and Rest change?' 'Of course', says Theaetetus. The EV accordingly concludes that some things will mix together (συμμείγνυσθαι) while others will not (252e).

This passage raises a difficulty. We have seen that all objects of knowledge (probably) 'change' in so far as they are known, and (certainly) are at rest *qua* objects of knowledge. We seem now to be talking about the concepts (or 'Kinds' as they are called at 253b—from the Platonic point of view, Forms) of Rest and Change. If we are talking about attribution, why should we not attribute Change to Rest and Rest to Change? Yet the EV seems to accept Theaetetus' verdict, and we shall find that he even uses the conclusion that Rest and Change do not mix together when engaged upon a different argument at 254d, and in a further argument at 255a appears to assume that they are not mutually predicable.

Moravcsik (45) takes the meaning to be that 'if there were a thoroughgoing universal mingling, then Rest and Motion could not be regarded as separate Forms. . . .

Motion and Rest could not be contradictories, and this is
absurd'. This is to abandon, of course, the idea that we
are simply concerned with predication. Runciman (94 ff.)
likewise abandons that idea. He considers first whether
Rest and Change are supposed not to combine 'because
Change must be changing and Rest must be at rest', and
then whether the point may be that they are not *entirely*
predicable' of each other. He concludes that 'Plato may
well have had in mind something of both trains of
thought . . . a sort of total supervention which would
involve the commingling of opposite natures and a total
mutual predication and identity'. But (i) when the EV
asks whether it is utterly impossible for Change to rest
or for Rest to change, he does not repeat Theaetetus'
word 'completely' from 252d6; (ii) even when full
account is taken of the 'completely', these interpretations
seem to involve putting a great deal of stress on the prefix
of ἐπικοινωνία so as to distinguish it, as referring to
'total supervention', from the κοινωνία of 251e which
simply meant 'communion'; in fact (iii), not only would
the supposition at 252d appear to be the direct opposite
of that at 251e, so that ἐπικοινωνία ought to mean the
same as κοινωνία—and we have seen good reason for
taking κοινωνία at 250b, 251e and 252b to refer simply
to attribution—but the natural way of taking 251d would
be to assume that ἐπικοινωνεῖν there means much the
same as μεταλαμβάνειν;[1] and finally (iv), one of Plato's
chief aims, as we have seen, is to distinguish predication
from identification, and Runciman's conclusion involves
accusing Plato, as he does in fact explicitly accuse him
(96), of 'appearing to perpetrate a confusion which it is

[1] See p. 107. [Cf. Marten, 214, n. 134 for a refutation of Runciman
along similar lines.]

his object to elucidate'. We may well look for a more plausible solution.

The answer is likely to be this. The word Change may stand for the concept of change, and Change in that sense may be described as unchanging. But Change as a common noun may be taken as designating particular instances of change, considered not collectively but severally;[1] and of them, of course, 'at rest' ('unchanging') could not be truly predicated. For Plato himself, Forms seem to have done service in both ways: as universals, and as the only true *designata* of common nouns—as paradigms.[2] Now when Theaetetus says that Change 'would come to a complete standstill', he is not simply confusing predication with identification, for if one essayed the impossible task of identifying the *concept* of change with the concept of rest, at least there is no reason to suppose that the disastrous result envisaged by

[1] As when we say, 'Change is a good thing.'
[2] See also pp. 122 n., 131, 142, 148ff., 160.
[Bluck's interpretation of Forms as combining the roles of universal and paradigm seems to me historically sound, as against R. E. Allen's exclusive support for the latter at the expense of the former. Philosophically true it may be that 'commutative universals or attributes clearly cannot be identified with standards or paradigms' (53); but is there any evidence for thinking that it was clear to Plato? In any case, Allen's own description of the Forms is little less equivocal (58): 'Like reflections, particulars differ in type from their originals; they share no common attribute; and yet they exhibit a fundamental community of character.' Bluck explored his hypothesis in relation to earlier dialogues in an article published in 1957, 'Forms as Standards': it is perhaps, however, fair to add that as his manuscript contained no reference anywhere to it, there may be points in it which he would no longer wish to endorse. See also the exchange between Mills (40 ff.) and Bluck ('Plato's Form of Equal') over 'the equals themselves' (αὐτὰ τὰ ἴσα, *Phaedo* 74c).

Kamlah believes that Plato drops his earlier view of the Forms as models (Urbilder) by the time of the *Sophist*, only to reintroduce a revised version of it in the *Timaeus*. He doesn't deal adequately with the difficulties which Bluck is concerned to explain. But perhaps Kamlah's somewhat unlikely thesis may be seen as further confirmation that Plato cannot be fitted without remainder into exclusive modern pigeonholes.]

Theaetetus would befall change. He is clearly treating 'Change' and 'Rest' in the other way, as denoting the several instances of change and rest. If they are regarded in this way, Change and Rest might still be described as 'Kinds'; but it is then true that they could not be attributed to one another. This interpretation has several important advantages over any other. It allows us to admit, simultaneously, (i) that the EV, even when he accepts Theaetetus' verdict, is thinking in terms of attribution, (ii) that the example does prove what it is meant to prove, that participation between Kinds is not always possible, and (iii) that it is nevertheless possible (as we know it must be) to attribute Rest to Change.

It may perhaps be tempting to some readers to suppose that Plato, by showing that to attribute Rest to Change *qua* paradigm virtually amounted to identification, intended to reduce to absurdity and to abolish the conception of Kinds as paradigms. But such a reading of the passage is not compatible with any reasonable interpretation of it in its dramatic setting; for if the argument is taken to be unsound because based on an unsatisfactory conception of a Kind, we are left without any satisfactory proof that Kinds will not always mix together. Furthermore the treatment of Change and Rest as common nouns is, as we have seen, quite legitimate. There is also some evidence that may suggest that Plato was not fully aware of the nature of the distinction between the two ways in which he had regarded Forms.

Had Plato been fully aware of the nature of that distinction, he might have been expected to make the EV ask here, not simply whether some or all of the Kinds will mix together, but also whether some of them will in one capacity but not in another. That he does not do so

is all the more striking in view of a passage some three
and a half Stephanus pages later (256b6–7), where the
EV, in reviewing the relationships between Change and
the other Kinds discussed, seems to hint that Change can,
after all, participate in Rest. This passage is best considered in its context; but the very fact that it is only a
hint suggests that Plato himself may have been puzzled,
and certainly no explanation is offered of the apparent
contradiction between the idea that Rest can be predicated of Change (as we know in any case that it can) and
the present passage. It may be added that that passage
(256b) lends no support to the view that we are at present
concerned with some sort of 'total supervention', for had
that been the case there would have been every need for
an explanation of the *apparent* discrepancy, and *no* reason
why such an explanation should not be given.[1]

3. CONCLUSION

The sort of 'account' of 'what is' that merely states what
it consists of is found still to leave unexplained the nature
of Being itself. From what the EV says at the beginning
of this section, we may infer perhaps that even the distinguishing mark which the EV offered to the materialists
and idealists could hardly count as a full explanation of
it.[2] However that may be, the EV does not pursue the
question what 'is' means beyond reasserting the independent existence of Being, and stating some puzzles about

[1] Confirmation of the possibility of taking Rest and Change in the way
here suggested may be found at 253e: see p. 131. Cf. also p. 113, n. 2.
[2] Possibly Plato still believed that understanding of the nature of any
Form was a matter of personal apprehension, and could not be con-
veyed by words, and that the man who had knowledge of a Form could
state a distinguishing mark of its instances, but could not put its nature
into a formula.

it which have a direct bearing on the main argument of the dialogue: (i) 'of its own nature' Being neither rests nor changes, and (ii) Being itself seems therefore not to conform to the notion that 'what is' consists of what is changing and of what is changeless. This has led to a discussion designed to elucidate the distinction between the 'proper nature' of a thing and its attributes. After mentioning the puzzle of 'one man with many names', the EV has shown that in some cases things like Change, Rest and Being (shortly to be called 'Kinds') will 'mix together': that is to say, in some cases a Kind or Form can have the quality of another Kind or Form as an attribute.

The next step in the main argument will be to illustrate such mixing by means of examples. We shall eventually find that as all Kinds can mix with Being without losing their identity, so all Kinds can mix with Otherness and be 'things that are not' without losing their identity or their share in Being.

DIALECTIC AND THE COMMUNION OF FORMS

I. VOWEL FORMS AND DISJUNCTIVE FORMS

After the agreement that some things will mix together and some will not, and before the detailed study of certain special relationships which is part of the main argument, the EV makes some general remarks about the procedure involved and the science to which it belongs. Since, he says, some things will mix together while others will not, we may find an analogy in the letters of the alphabet, some of which do not fit together while others do; and at 253a4–6 he adds, 'But the vowels stand out conspicuously from the rest, forming a sort of bond running through the whole system, in such a way that without the help of one of them it is impossible to fit one of the other letters to any other.' He then suggests that just as a special art is needed if one is to know which letters can 'have communion' (κοινωνεῖν) with which, or if one is to know, in the case of high and low musical notes, which will 'mix together' and which will not, so a special art is needed if one is to be able to show correctly which 'Kinds' (γένη) harmonize (συμφωνεῖν) with which and which are incompatible (ἄλληλα οὐ δέχεται), 'and moreover whether there are, running through all, some [Kinds?] that hold them together, so that they can mix together, and again, where there are divisions, whether running through wholes (δι' ὅλων) there are others responsible for the division' (253c).

The important question here is precisely what Plato

is suggesting in his description of vowels, and where the point of comparison lies between them and the elements (clearly supposed to be analogous to vowels) which 'hold Kinds together so that they can mix together'. A great deal more has sometimes been made of this passage than the text warrants, and Plato's meaning is probably quite simple and very different from what has generally been supposed.

To judge from what we discover later in the dialogue, what Plato has in mind as 'responsible for divisions' must be, or at least include, Otherness[1]—which for Plato would almost certainly be a Form.[2] This fact, combined with the letters analogy—since vowels are themselves letters—makes it highly probable that the things which enable Kinds to mix together are, for Plato, Forms. But it is not obvious precisely what it is that they achieve, nor how they achieve it. For if the vowel-elements and the Kinds that they enable to mix are all Forms, we are dealing not merely with language, but with the structure of reality, with relationships between the Forms themselves.[3]

When Forms mix together, this normally means, as we have seen, that one of them (at least) can be predicated of the other, and although Plato is interested in language only in so far as it provides clues to the nature of reality, it is reasonable to suppose that as one vowel Form, at any rate, he has in mind a Form answering to the 'is' of predication. However, this 'is' is represented in Platonic language, as Ackrill has shown, by the formula of par-

---

[1] See p. 123.

[2] See p. 165 f.

[3] Since we are concerned here with what the passage was meant to convey to readers acquainted with Platonism, it will be convenient to speak in what follows of the Kinds, vowel-elements and elements 'responsible for divisions' as Forms, no matter how 'the Sophist' or anyone else might be expected to understand them.

taking or participating, and Ackrill (1) holds that partaking
is not the name of a Form. But although we hear nothing
of a Form of Partaking, we have already heard a good
deal about Being; and if this is the Form in question, the
remarks about vowels are not merely incidental, but are
relevant to the main argument. If, moreover, Plato had
not clearly distinguished between the existential and the
copulative senses of 'to be', this will account for the failure to mention a particular Form answering to the latter
sense alone.[1]

   If there is a Form of Being which answers to both these
senses, then Form A, which is a character, will owe the
fact that it is a character to participation in Being. Now
if Form A can have something predicated of it—for
instance, the fact that it is other than Form B—it will
have communion with the Form to which the predicate
refers, in this instance Otherness. But such communion
presupposes that A participates in Being. A cannot have
communion with any other Form X without participating
in Being, for if it did not so participate, there would *be*
no A to have communion with X; and hence participation in Being may be regarded as logically prior to
having communion with any other Form. It may well be
in this sense that Plato is thinking of Being as making
'mixing together' possible. By pervading all the Forms,
it enables them to be what they are; and it is because of
this that a Form can mix together with other Forms and
reflect their characters as attributes of itself.

----

[1] Although Ackrill's intention is to show that three senses of 'is' are
distinguished in the *Sophist*, he does not achieve his goal. He rightly
treats the difference between identity and attribution as crucial to the
argument of the dialogue, but cannot be said to have established an
existential usage. [In fact, in as far as all statements with 'is' can be equally
well represented by the formula of participation, it is perhaps more
appropriate to talk of different *usages* of 'is' rather than different *meanings*.]

Peck's interpretation of the *Sophist* rests heavily on the view that the copulative sense is never totally absent from the verb 'to be' in the dialogue. But his argument that Being is not a Form at all but more of a deceptive 'appearance' (φάντασμα), as also is 'what is not' (51), falls foul of the present passage about vowel Forms (among others). Because the statement 'Change is' (κίνησις ἔστιν), for example, is really abbreviated from 'Change is Change', he argues (51) that 'with τὸ ὄν there is no common attribution, for τὸ ὄν . . . has a different content and value in each case', and so is 'an invalid γένος'. According to Peck, Plato's aim is to reduce the terms 'is' and 'is not' altogether to their specific instances. Thus of 257b ff. he says: 'Instead of speaking of ὄν and μὴ ὄν, the EV now speaks of μέγα and μὴ μέγα, καλόν and μὴ καλόν, etc.' (Once again he is probably right to stress the predicative role of the verb: see p. 162.)

There are a number of strong reasons against Peck's basic thesis, however. One is that there is no reason to suppose that Plato would have been in any way reluctant to posit Forms corresponding to 'incomplete' predicates: witness the Forms Equality (ἰσότης) and Largeness (μέγεθος) in the *Phaedo* (74c, 102d), the instances of which are necessarily relational.[1] Another is that at 257b ff., so far from speaking of 'not large' (μὴ μέγα), etc. *instead of* speaking of 'what is not' (μὴ ὄν), the EV leads *from* his discussion of 'the not-large' and the like *to* the conclusion that ' "what is not" in the same way both was and is a "thing that is not", a single Form to be counted among the many things that are' (258c).[2] But the present passage, with its strong emphasis on the fact that cer-

---

[1] See also p. 142f.
[2] Cf. p. 161.

tain Forms are in some sense actual and universal causes of mixture and separation, is itself adequate reason for thinking that Plato was giving to Being and Other-ness, if we have rightly identified these as the relevant Forms, a status higher than was usually recognized rather than emptying them of all content.

It is misleading to describe a vowel Form, as Moravcsik does (49), as a 'connecting' Form. Moravcsik (50) criti-cizes Cornford on the ground that 'in his scheme two Forms blend or do not blend depending on how they compare, and not on account of their relations to a third connecting Form'.[1] On the present explanation of the analogy, there is no need, when considering whether Forms combine, to consider 'their relations to a third connecting Form', in the first place because all Forms participate in Being and all are related to it in the same way, and secondly because the 'being' of things is simply the *sine qua non* of *any* characterization, and has nothing to do with the question whether two particular Forms combine or not.

Moravcsik seems to think of Being as somehow sand-wiched between two Forms that combine, as a vowel is sandwiched between two consonants; he gives as an illustration (49) the way in which mortar connects bricks. But there is no justification in the text for this, unless we press the fact that a vowel comes between the two con-sonants that 'fit together'. This fact is probably extra-neous to the purpose of the analogy. It is not even specially mentioned. On the contrary, at 253a we have a simile of a bond running through all the letters, and

[1] Cornford does not explain the vowel analogy. He merely says (262) that 'pervasive Forms are obviously the meanings of certain words used in affirmative statements . . . the meanings of the word "is", which we shall distinguish presently'.

correspondingly at 253c the expressions 'running through all' and 'holding the Kinds together', the main emphasis apparently being on all-pervasiveness. And at 253b the reference to high and low notes which will mix together could at least as easily be an allusion to a chord as to a succession of notes. Had mixing depended on *special* relationships between *three* Forms, we might have expected some emphasis on a vowel Form's *intermediate* position; but at 253b the EV merely uses the musical metaphor of 'harmonizing' (συμφωνεῖν). Since all Forms in any case must have the same relationship as each other to Being, Being's function as a vowel Form cannot determine which Kinds harmonize with which. It simply enables *every* Form to have *some* character, with the result that some of them may mix.

There is therefore no need to worry with Runciman (105) about 'the faint aroma of a regress about any assertion that two Forms are connected by a third', or to try to avoid it by saying with Moravcsik (49) that 'the connecting material is of a different type'. There is no question of a regress, not because the Form of Being is different in kind from other Forms, but because it does not connect in the way in which mortar connects bricks.[1]

On the present interpretation it is reasonable, when considering whether two Forms combine, to compare them directly. It is likewise reasonable, when it is found that two Forms do combine, to express that conclusion simply by saying that '*A* partakes of *B*', without referring

---

[1] [There is a residual problem here, of course. Even if the role of Being is simply to enable a Form to have *some* character, so long as Being is itself a Form with the rest, what enables it in its turn to have the character it does? Bluck's interpretation of similar problems elsewhere in the dialogue in terms of paradigm Forms would also go a long way towards explaining why Plato failed to see this difficulty as crucial. Cf. p. 113, n. 2.]

to any third Form. Indeed the EV himself does so (e.g. 255b). There is no need to suppose that such a statement would be short for 'A partakes of Being in relation to B', as Runciman does when he translates (112) 'Theaetetus sits' into 'Theaetetus partakes of Being in relation to Sitting'. In such a formulation 'in relation to' would be inexplicable.

Moravcsik (42) treats Otherness and Sameness, as well as Being, as 'Forms whose primary function is to make connections possible'. But Otherness must be the Form, or one of the Forms, 'responsible for division'. Certainly in the statement 'A is other than B' Otherness cannot be said to be enabling A and B to mix together, if 'mixing together' implies that the one can be predicated of the other. In 253c3, in view of the reference to Divisions, the 'wholes' there will be complex Forms; the divisions will be between their 'parts' or species, which are other than each other; and what is responsible for this situation can only be the Form of Otherness. But the text does not suggest that Forms 'responsible for divisions' are vowel Forms, rather that they are to be contrasted with those Forms which make mixing possible.

Cornford (262) takes the vowel Forms to be 'the meanings of the word "is", which we shall distinguish presently'. This will include the meaning of the identi-tative 'is', the Form of Sameness. But it is difficult to see how Sameness can be made to fit the description of a vowel Form at 253c1–3. It is all-pervasive in the sense that everything is the same as itself (256a7–8), and if two things that are identical with one another could be said to mix, it might be regarded as responsible for the mixing. But there is no such instance of two things that are identical with one another being described as mixing.

Moreover, the question 'whether there are some things that hold the Kinds together' suggests that the EV is thinking of Forms which are involved in every mixture.

There seems, in fact, to be only one obvious vowel Form, Being, and only one Form obviously responsible for divisions, Otherness. And indeed the use of the plural in the text need not mean that there actually is more than one Form of each kind. The EV is not stating a doctrine, but indicating what it would be desirable to know; and the plural may have been suggested in the case of the vowel Forms by the nature of the analogy, since there is a plurality of vowels. That Plato had in mind just these two Forms, Being and Otherness, is perhaps all the more likely in view of the fact that they are the Forms corresponding to the senses of 'is' and 'is not' in which he is particularly interested.

The present interpretation of the function of a vowel Form and the function of a disjunctive Form has no implausible metaphysical consequences. We do not have to imagine, within the spaceless realm of Forms, two Forms somehow related to each other indirectly, through the agency of a mediating Form. All that is involved is that each Form, precisely because it *is* something, is capable of being compared (directly) with other Forms, and of being found to manifest, either in itself or in its relationships, the natures of some of the others; and precisely because every Form is *other* than every other Form, there will be natural divisions between them, though in no case such a division as could cause complete isolation, since every Form partakes of Being. This conception is an improvement on the theory attributed to the 'Friends of Forms'.

2. DIVIDING BY KINDS

Having expressed the need for a special science to study 'mixing', the EV goes on, 'Dividing by Kinds and not thinking that the same Form (εἶδος) is another one or another one the same, we shall surely say belongs to the science of Dialectic' (253d). He then adds the following statement:

So he who can do this clearly perceives one Form entirely extended through many things, though each one (ἑνὸς ἑκάστου) lies apart, and many Forms, other than each other, embraced (περιεχομένας) from without by one; and again one Form throughout many wholes connected into a unity, and many Forms apart, entirely distinct. This means knowing how to discern, Kind by Kind, how each set of things can or cannot have communion. (253d–e)

Cornford translates the first sentence here, 'Dividing according to Kinds . . . is not that the business of the science of Dialectic?' That rendering (and Taylor's is similar) might suggest that Division is the *whole* of the business of Dialectic. But Moravcsik (51) points out that the two are not identified, and it is safer to assume with him that Division is only part of the business of Dialectic.

Moravcsik himself, however, goes too far when he says (52) that ability to divide 'is clearly a prerequisite to the ability to tell which Forms combine'. The general sense of what we are told is that the man who can divide correctly can discern the genus-species relationships within the world of Forms, and that is the same thing as having a knowledge of what combines with what. Thus we seem to be told that ability to divide presupposes a knowledge of what can or cannot have communion, not the converse. Moreover, such conclusions as are reached in this dialogue about combination are reached without the aid of Division, or any indication that the EV has done his dividing in advance. The two skills belong to the same science and no doubt go hand in hand, but it would appear that the study of communion is practised for the sake of Division, rather than *vice versa*.

The first half of the next sentence (253d5–8) presents no great difficulty. The description is clearly a description of a part of a genus-species hierarchy within the world of Forms. But two points may be noted where Cornford (267) is perhaps wrong.[1]

He takes 'clearly perceives' to allude to the dialectician's discovery, 'by intuition', of a generic Form. But this verb also has another object, the 'many Forms embraced by one'. It is more likely that the EV is talking here not about the dialectician actually engaged upon the work of Collection, but about the picture of the interrelations of the Form-complex which the man who is capable of dividing must possess in his mind. If he is *ex hypothesi* capable of dividing, he must 'see' or 'discern' this picture before his mind's eye; and just because he sees it, he must have a knowledge of what combines with what, for that is virtually the same thing.

The other point is that Cornford takes 'one Form extended throughout many things' to mean 'one Form extended throughout many Forms', rejecting Campbell's assumption that the 'many things' are 'individuals' on the ground that 'the whole procedure deals with Forms only'

---

[1] [Sayre is right (186 ff.) that Division in Plato does not conform strictly to the Aristotelian rules for genus-species relationships; but it is doubtful whether anyone supposed that it did. For example, see the discussion of the seventh series in the appendix to chapter 1 above. Sayre himself can still talk (179) of the 'tree of division'; like Cornford, he interprets 253d–e as referring directly to Collection and Division.]

(267, n. 2).[1] But the Greek word (πολλῶν) is neuter, as the appositional ἑνὸς ἑκάστου shows, whereas the word for a Form in this sentence is feminine (ἰδέα), so that the reference *ought* to be to many particulars;[2] and there is no reason to suppose that the EV is not referring to the particulars subsumed under a Form, since a Collection of particulars might well precede a Collection of Forms and subsequent Division (cf. Hackforth, 142 f.).

The 'many Forms embraced by one', as is clear from 250e where the same word meaning 'embraced' was used, will be many Forms which all participate in one Form; and as we are talking about the man who is able to divide, these participating Forms will be species of which the 'embracing' Form is the genus.

The second half of this sentence, 'One Form throughout many wholes connected into a unity, and many Forms apart, entirely distinct', has given rise to various interpretations.

Taylor (157n.) takes 'many Forms apart' to be 'such "categorial characters" as *rest* and *motion, identity* and *otherness*, which are direct contraries', and believes that 'consequently the "single form pervading a multitude of wholes" will also be a categorial character, like e.g. *being* or *sameness*, or *difference*. . . . But *same* and *different* are not . . . *genera*'. But 'apart' and 'distinct' need not mean 'contrary to one another', any more than 'other than each other' did in 253d7. Again the 'one Form' is said to pervade *many* wholes, not *all* wholes, as we might expect

---

[1] [Campbell's interpretation (145) is supported by others; for references see Meinhardt (40, n. 2–5). Meinhardt himself argues that Plato is here concerned exclusively with Forms, on the evidence of *Republic* 511b, where dialectic is explicitly stated to make no use at all of sensible objects.]

[2] [Bluck's statement of the point is less elliptical than Runciman's (62).]

if Being, Sameness or Otherness were meant. Nor does this explanation account for the use of the word 'wholes'.

Moravcsik's view (52) is similar. He takes the 'one Form' to be 'a vowel-Form which is incomplete in itself and is completed by a plurality of Forms which it pervades and connects', because 'the Greek is here similar to the language of 253a4–5, 253c1–2, 255e3–6, and 259a5–6'. But those passages are concerned with what is 'pervading all things', the present one with what is 'pervading many wholes'. In 253c3 we find the expression 'through wholes', but there the reference is to complex Form-wholes which are divided. Moravcsik does not explain the use of the word 'wholes' here. Certainly Plato would have departed a long way from his earlier conception of Forms if he could think of one as 'incomplete in itself' and 'completed' by other Forms.

Cornford (267), unlike Taylor and Moravcsik, allows that this part of the sentence has some connection with Division. But he assumes that it describes the results of Division practised for the purpose of defining something. The 'many Forms apart' are 'the indivisible species in which Division terminates', and 'the term "wholes" is applied to the many (specific) Forms because, now that they have been completely defined, they are seen as complexes: each is a whole whose parts are enumerated in the defining formula, such as "Man is the rational biped Animal"'. But there has been no mention here of defining; and this explanation, which identifies the 'many wholes' with the 'many Forms apart' and treats them as 'indivisible species', involves taking the 'wholes' here very differently from the 'wholes' of 253c3. Those 'wholes', as Cornford says (262), are 'Forms considered as complexes divisible into parts (or species)'.

A much simpler solution than any of these is available.
It may be illustrated for ease of reference as follows.

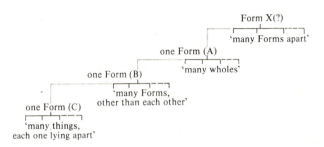

The 'one Form throughout many wholes connected into
a unity' (Form A) and that by which 'many Forms, other
than each other, are embraced' (Form B) will simply be
more comprehensive Forms than the 'one Form extended
through many things' (Form C) already mentioned. The
'many wholes' will themselves be generic (and therefore
divisible) Forms, though now subsumed under a higher
genus. We may postulate that the 'many Forms apart' are
Forms which, though distinct from one another (and
therefore separable from one another by Division), can
be collaterally subsumed under one higher generic Form
(X). This at least is suggested by the similarity of the
expression 'apart, entirely distinct' to the expressions
applied to the other groups of collateral entities, 'each
one lying apart' and 'other than each other'; for there is
no need for it to mean any more than they do.[1]

[1] The word πάντη occurs in 253d6 (where both Cornford and Taylor
render it 'everywhere') as well as in d9 (where Cornford renders it
'entirely', Taylor 'wholly'). I have kept to 'entirely' in both places, but it
is possible that for 'entirely distinct', 'everywhere separate' should be
substituted.
[Crombie's interpretation (418) follows similar lines, but is based on a

If these 'many Forms apart' can be subsumed under
one Form (X), they are probably to be thought of as
collateral with the 'one Form' (A) of which the 'many
wholes' are species. It is also possible that Form C should
be regarded as itself one of the 'many Forms other than
each other', and Form B as one of the 'many wholes'.
This is all the more probable if the 'many Forms apart'
are thought of as collateral with Form A, for then the
EV will have been thinking of a regular 'upward' pro-
gression. But this is a matter of little importance. What
matters is that we are most probably concerned with
genera and species throughout.[1]

One point of considerable importance arises out of the
EV's final words here, which Cornford (263) renders
thus: 'That means knowing how to distinguish, Kind by
Kind, in what ways the several Kinds can or can not
combine'. In the Greek, 'Kind by Kind' (κατὰ γένος)
comes *after* ἕκαστα, which therefore (being on its own)
seems unlikely to mean 'the several Kinds'. On the
other hand, we cannot understand 'Forms', as the word

rather forced gradation of meaning between the verbs translated above
by 'extended' ('permeates'—Crombie), 'embraced', and 'connected'. He,
however, extends the chain to cover universal, but purely formal properties 'such as existing, being one, being self-same' (Form A and the
'many Forms apart', presumably).]
    [1] [Meinhardt's book on participation in Plato is largely an attempt to
elucidate this single passage, and is therefore a much fuller treatment
than Bluck offers here. It may well be that Plato's tantalizingly terse
description here suggests some schematic formulation of the task of
dialectic current in the Academy, as Meinhardt believes (38), but it
cannot be said that he has settled the issue, or indeed that he is any more
convincing than Bluck's less technical interpretation. 'Codeterminance'
(*Mitkonstitutivität*) may be a useful modern synonym for 'participation',
but it is no more than that, and incidentally requires the inversion of subject and (indirect) object. Moreover, Meinhardt's exposition is often
tendentious, and in my opinion throws little or no extra light on the
many crucial problems associated with participation in the theory of
Forms.]

for Form in this sentence is not neuter but feminine
(ἰδέα). The neuter plural ἕκαστα would seem to mean
'each set of particulars',[1] especially as πολλῶν in 253d6,
as we have seen, almost certainly means 'many particulars'. Now if this is what it means, what the EV is saying
in 253e1–2 is that to discern the genus-species relationships within the realm of Forms is to be able to distinguish, Kind by Kind, how *each set of particular things* can
or cannot have communion. This implies that if two
Forms have communion with one another, the two
corresponding sets of particulars can have it too, and
that if the Forms cannot have communion with one
another, then neither can the sets of particulars. But this
could only be true if the Forms are regarded not as
concepts, but as *designata* of common nouns which are
also used in reference to particulars, considered severally.
This is precisely the way in which it was found necessary
to understand Change and Rest at 252d[2] and the finding
here and the finding there may be held to lend each other
mutual support.

3. CONCLUSION

It has appeared that Being is compared to a vowel because
without partaking of Being Forms could have no communion with each other, just as there could be no combination of letters into a syllable without a vowel; and it
has appeared that Otherness is the Form responsible for
the natural divisions between things, for the separateness
of independent natures (or Forms). It will follow from

---

[1] [More accurately than Schipper (43), who translates 'each of the
particulars'.]

[2] See p. 113ff.

the former conclusion that whereas a Form, through partaking of Otherness, may be said 'not to be' X, Y or Z, its 'not-being', so far from meaning that it has no being, is possible only because it *does* partake of Being; likewise Otherness or Not-being itself must partake of Being. The remarks about the vowel and disjunctive Forms are made casually, apropos of the science which has to do with the 'mixing' of Forms, and the implications are not explicitly drawn or intended to be recognized as yet, but will be drawn out and clarified in what follows. They will also be found to accord with what is said about falsity.

The brief passage 253d1–e2 has been dealt with at length because of the variety of interpretations to which it has given rise and its intrinsic importance, but it has no direct bearing on the main subject of discussion. We have however already noted the possible implication that particulars can or cannot have communion with one another according to whether or not the corresponding Forms have communion with one another; and there will be occasion, later on, in considering the explanation of false statement, to recall the words used by the EV in connection with Division (253d), 'not thinking that the same Form is another one or another one the same'.[1]

---

[1] [These paragraphs contain some of the few hints Bluck has left us of how he would have interpreted the discussion later in the dialogue concerning false statement.]

HOW FIVE IMPORTANT 'KINDS' RELATE

I. FIVE NATURES PROVED DISTINCT

At 254b–c the EV reverts to the main line of the discussion, which was interrupted at 252e. Now that it has
been agreed that some Kinds will have communion with
each other while others will not, he proposes to consider

not all the Forms, in case we become confused among many,
but a selection from among those that are said to be most
important: considering first what each of them is like, and
then how they stand in regard to the power to have communion with one another, so that even if we cannot grasp 'what
is' and 'what is not' with complete clarity, at least we shall
not have failed to discuss them fully, so far as the character of
the present enquiry permits, to see whether after all there is
some means by which we may assert that 'what is not' really
is something that 'is not' and still come off unscathed.

It is interesting that what are called Kinds (γένη) in 254b
appear to be the same things as are called Forms (εἴδη)
in 254c. Coming as it does immediately after the discussion of Dialectic, this passage seems to be a clear
indication that the reader acquainted with Platonic doctrine should interpret what follows in terms of Platonic
Forms.

The 'power (δύναμις) to have communion' is an
expression that recalls the mark of 'things that are'
suggested by the EV to the materialists and the idealists,
'the power to affect or be affected'; for not only is the
word for 'power' the same, but we found that having an

attribute amounted to being affected,[1] and we have also found that having communion seems normally to imply attribution.[2] Yet we can hardly suppose that Rest and Change, for example, in having communion with Being, are affected by Being and therefore 'changed'. The attributes involved in the communion which the EV now discusses are permanent attributes, and it would seem that the possessors of them cannot be in any way changed by having them. There is no real difficulty here, however, for the EV has never said that being affected *always* implies being changed. He only suggested that if to be known was to be affected, *that* would amount to being changed (248e);[3] and 'being known' (by X, or Y, or Z) is not a permanent characteristic. The power to have communion probably connotes the power to affect or be affected, but this need not imply change.

There follows a series of proofs showing in each case that the Forms discussed have separate identity. But these proofs also have another aim, obviously of no less importance than the first, namely the elucidation of the difference between predication and identification. Considerable stress is laid on this problem throughout the section.

Argument 1: 254d4–12. The EV takes Being, Rest and Change, and argues thus: 'Two of them, we say, cannot mix (ἀμείκτω) with one another. . . . But Being can mix (μεικτόν) with both, for they both, I suppose, *are*. . . . So that these prove to be three.'

(*a*) *Runciman's explanation.*[4] The reference to the agreement that 'two of these cannot mix' is a reference to 252d,

---

[1] See p. 97 ff.   [2] See pp. 107 ff., 111 ff.   [3] See p. 95.
[4] The criticisms offered in this section of the explanations of others

where Runciman took Plato to be thinking of total predication and of identity.[1] This time he declares that the
word ἀμείκτω in 254d7 'without question expresses a
relation of non-identity . . . it is the non-identity of
Change and Rest which is reasserted without any assertion that mutual predication would be impossible' (96).
But as Moravcsik (43) points out, if 'cannot mix' means
'is not identical with', this 'would force us to read
"Being mixes with both" as "Being is identical with
both" '.[2]

(b) *Moravcsik's explanation.* Moravcsik (45) 'cannot regard
μεικτόν as indicating predication'. He holds that Rest and
Change do not mix 'in the sense that they are opposites',
and that 'Being "mixes" with both in the sense that it is
not an opposite of either and that it "surrounds" both'.
These last words allude to the suggestion at 250b that
Rest and Change are 'surrounded' or 'embraced' (περιεχ-
ομένην) by Being; and this 'surrounding' Moravcsik (44)
takes to indicate that 'Being includes Rest and Motion[3]
in the sense that whatever is either in motion or at rest
must necessarily exist, and that Being is in no way contrary to either Rest or Motion'.

But at 250b their being 'surrounded' by Being was
given as the justification for saying that Rest and Change

have been so arranged that the reader who wishes to do so can easily skip
them and pass on to what is presented as probably the best explanation
of each argument.

[1] Runciman 94–6; see above p. 112 ff.

[2] Moravcsik also says that it would make the argument circular, but it
would only do this if the EV was offering a proof that Change and Rest
must be distinct from each other. It is more likely, however, that the
point at issue here is the separate existence of the third Kind, Being.
Change and Rest are probably assumed to be distinct on the grounds
that they are complete opposites: see subsection (c) below.

[3] 'Motion' is Moravcsik's rendering of κίνησις ('Change').

themselves (not their extensions) 'are', and nothing was said about non-opposition between them and Being.[1] There is no reason to suppose that opposites cannot mix simply because they are opposites. Sameness and Otherness are opposites, but they partake of each other (cf. 255e, 256a), and presumably must count not only as having communion with one another (cf. 254b), but as among the 'some things' which it was agreed at 252e must 'mix together'; for the discussion as to whether anything could be 'attached' to anything else was clearly a preliminary to the present discussion, and the conclusion that some things 'mix together' was picked up immediately prior to the present series of arguments in the words, 'Since then it has been agreed that some of the Kinds will have communion with one another . . .' (254b). Indeed since partaking of Being means that a thing *is* (256a1, 256d9),[2] and we are now told that if Rest and Change *are*, they mix with Being, partaking of something would seem to imply ability to mix with it. The example of Sameness and Otherness makes it most unlikely that Rest and Change do not mix simply because they are opposites.

(*c*) *Suggested solution*. The words at 254d10 'for they both, I suppose, are' seem clearly to indicate that Rest and Change mix with Being in the sense that it can be predicated of them. The assertion is similar to the assertion at 250b that we can say that they both are because they both have communion with Being.[3] The proposition

---

[1] See p. 103 f. The word περιεχομένας occurs at 253d, 'many Forms embraced by one', again without reference to particular instances or to non-opposition.

[2] See p. 151 f.

[3] See p. 103 f.

that they cannot mix with one another will therefore
mean that they cannot be predicated of one another. We
have already discussed the problem raised by this assumption at 252d, and found that there is no difficulty if Rest
and Change are being treated as *designata* of common
nouns and virtually paradigm cases.[1]

The EV now repeats that conclusion, and argues that
Being cannot be identical with Rest or Change because
it can be truly predicated of them, whereas they cannot
be truly predicated of each other. That Rest and Change
are not identical with each other is assumed, probably because it was agreed at 250a that they are
complete opposites.[2] Therefore these are three different
Kinds.

As it was Theaetetus who originally made the assumption that Rest and Change could not be truly predicated
of one another (252d), it might be tempting to regard the
present argument as simply an *argumentum ad hominem*,
especially as a different argument for the independent
existence of Being, one not involving this assumption,
was presented at 250a–b. But the same assumption is
made again at 255a,[3] and the series of arguments as a
whole seems intended to be valid. As we have seen, there
is a sense in which Rest and Change cannot be truly predicated of each other, whereas there is no sense of Rest
and Change in which Being cannot be truly predicated of
them. The present proof is needed, despite the argument
at 250a–b, for the sake of the completeness of the series,
and it is not inappropriate that the method of proof
should be varied.

[1] See p. 111 ff.
[2] See p. 103. Being was found in 250b to be a *third* thing.
[3] The strong hint at 256b that in one sense this assumption is not true
is discussed on p. 152 f.

Argument 2: 255a4–b6. The EV next argues that neither
Sameness nor Otherness[1] can be identified with either
Rest or Change. The following translation and the ex-
planatory comments added in square brackets are based
on what seems to be the best interpretation of a difficult
passage. Alternatives are discussed below and in the
appendix to this chapter.

But certainly Change and Rest are [identical with] neither
Other nor the Same.—How so?—Whatever we say that *both*
Change *and* Rest *are* [e.g. 'other' (than *X*) or 'the same' (as *Y*)],
neither of them can *be* [identical with] that thing.—Why?
(255a4–9)—Because [if Change or Rest is identified with e.g.
Other or the Same, and so predicated of both Change and
Rest], Change will rest *and moreover* Rest will change; for in
both cases[2] [but say, if Rest is identified with the Other],
whichever one of them [Change] becomes [identical with]
the other [Rest, through having it as an attribute] will *moreover* force the other [Rest] to turn into the opposite of *its* own
nature, through having come to partake of *its* opposite
[Change, which has been found to be identical with Rest,
and so may be regarded in its turn as the mutual attribute].
(255a10–b1)—Quite so.—But both partake of the Same and
the Other.—Yes.—Let us not, then, say that Change, or Rest
either, is [identical with] the Same or the Other.

255a10–b1 has been translated in many different ways,
but fortunately the difficulties do not affect the main argument of the dialogue. The above rendering may be called

---

[1] 'Sameness' and 'Otherness' seems a legitimate way of rendering
ταὐτόν and θάτερον, on the assumption that these are Forms. But they
may also be called 'the Same' and '(the) Other', which in some deliberately
ambiguous contexts is a necessary rendering.

[2] Literally, 'in regard to both', i.e. (as explained in what follows) whichever one be first supposed to have become its opposite. Cf. ἀμφοτέρως,
243e5.

version 1. Cornford gives what is perhaps a simpler rendering (version 2):

Because Motion would then be at rest, and Rest in motion; for whichever of the two (Motion or Rest) becomes applicable to both (by being identified with either Sameness or Difference which *are* applicable to both) will force the other (Rest or Motion) to change to the contrary of its own nature, as thus coming to partake of its contrary.

Whereas version 1 made the conjunction 'for' (a11) introduce the reason why *both* (Change and Rest) will undergo a reversal of nature if *either* is identified with a mutual attribute,[1] version 2 (Cornford) omits all reference to a double paradox. It makes the sentence an explanation simply of why the identification of either of the pair (say Rest) with the mutual attribute entails a contradiction in that it involves the reversal of the nature of the other (Change).[2]

Whichever of the versions we choose, and even if we take μετασχὸν τοῦ ἐναντίου (b1) to mean 'partaking of contrariety'[3] rather than 'having come to partake of its opposite', the argument certainly implies that if Rest or Change has its opposite predicated of it, it must reverse its nature. Some commentators again try to avoid this suggestion.

[1] On this view, no explanation is actually offered of why the *first* reversal of nature results (e.g. that if Rest is identified with the mutual attribute, Change will take on the nature of Rest), but only of why this first reversal entails the second (that Rest will in turn take on the nature of Change). But a similar assumption was put forward and accepted without explanation at 252d.

[2] [This is of course all that is necessary to establish the separateness of the four Kinds in question. See my note on Cornford in the appendix to this chapter.]

[3] This is hardly plausible in view of the preceding τοὐναντίον, but see appendix to this chapter for version 3.

(a) *Moravcsik's explanation.* 'Surely', says Moravcsik (46), 'mere predication would not change the nature of Rest into that of its opposite. Plato recognizes that the Same and the Other are all-pervasive and that they partake of each other. But this apparently does not affect their own natures.' He therefore suggests taking 255a7 to mean that whatever we 'apply in common *in the same sense only*' to Change and Rest, i.e. 'not as a name to one and as a description to the other', cannot be identical with either. Same and Other, he argues (47), *are* applied to both only in the same sense, i.e. as relational predicates: but if, for example, Rest were similarly applicable to both Rest and Change only in the same sense, 'then it must be the name of both since it is the name of one. This would indeed make Motion take up the nature of its opposite, namely, Rest.'[1] He takes the passage to be explaining the double paradox, and interprets the argument as follows: if e.g. Rest applies to Change as a name, it will become Change, and because it will therefore be impossible to distinguish the two, Change will also take up the nature of Rest.

However, the text requires that the one causes the reversal of the nature of the other by making that other 'partake of its opposite', which can hardly refer to being called by the name of its opposite.[2] Further, Moravcsik's

[1] [Moravcsik seems to ignore the fact that if e.g. Rest were identical with the Same, which is the very point at issue, then since the Same (like Other) applies to both Rest and Change as relational predicate, Rest could not be said to apply 'in the same sense only' as a name. It (and therefore the Same too) would apply as both name and relational predicate in one case, and as relational predicate alone in the other. Cf. Berger's slightly different statement of the same point (72 f.), and also his criticism (71) that Moravcsik's interpretation confuses Form and linguistic expression.]

[2] Moravcsik says (46): 'We are told that if either of the two would become the other then it would force the other to change its nature into that of its opposite, since this would have a share in it.' But it is not clear

explanation as to why, if *one* of the two 'became' the other in this way, *both* should change their natures, is unsatisfactory. 'One could not distinguish Rest and Motion', he says (47). But one could not distinguish them only because they would either both be Rest or both be Change (Motion); the fact that Change acquired a new name, Rest, might affect the nature of Rest, but there is no reason to suppose that it would alter the nature of Change.

(*b*) *Runciman's explanation.* Runciman does not indicate exactly how he would translate the passage, but he takes it (97) as claiming that 'if either Change or Rest is identical with Identity or Difference, the other of the pair must come to partake of its opposite'. He holds that 'partake' (μετασχόν) here must represent 'a stronger sense of participation than corresponds precisely to the copula as used in ordinary language'. As at 252d,[1] he thinks Plato must have in mind 'a sort of commingling which Forms which are opposite to each other by nature cannot undergo in relation to each other', though 'whether what Plato has in mind is a blending amounting more to identity or more to total predication it seems impossible to say' (98).

But again as at 252d, such an interpretation attributes to Plato the very confusion between predication and identification which it is his aim to dispel. That this is his aim is clear not only from what has preceded, but from 255b3, where the assertion that both (Rest and Change) 'partake' (μετέχετον) of the Same and the Other is

from this *what* he supposes would have a share in what, and in any case the point is ignored altogether in his later reconstruction of the argument.
[1] See p. 135, n. 1. above.

clearly to be contrasted with the conclusion that neither is identical with either the Same or the Other. Furthermore, this assertion at 255b3 makes it extremely difficult to see how the same verb at 255b1 could denote the sort of 'total supervention' that Runciman suggests; for there can be no question at 255b3 of identity or total predication, and the verb can hardly be used in radically different senses within three lines.

(c) *Suggested solution*. While it is difficult to decide exactly how the passage should be translated, the general sense is clear, and the difficulty as to why Change or Rest should reverse its nature if its opposite is predicated of it is at least explained if we recognize that Rest and Change are being treated not as concepts, but as *designata* of common nouns or standard instances, as in the previous argument. Regarded in this way, neither Rest nor Change could be predicated of both Rest and Change without in either case causing a reversal of nature.[1] But Same and Other can be predicated of both without any such consequences. Therefore both Rest and Change are distinct from Sameness and Otherness.

Two further points require comment here. First, Peck argues (*CQ* 1952, 47) that 'same' and 'other' are incomplete predicates, and cannot therefore be legitimately treated as common attributes of Change and Rest. But Plato may

---

[1] See p. 113f. 'Plato recognizes', says Moravcsik (46), 'that the Same and the Other . . . partake of each other. But this apparently does not affect their own natures.' But in their case it is true of both the concepts and the instances that they are the same as themselves and other than each other.

[Berger's attempt (76) to refute Moravcsik on this point by reference to 256d-e is a non sequitur, and is further weakened by Bluck's comments on the distinction between proper nature and attribute (see further p. 153; cf. p. 102).]

well have considered that the various respects or relationships in which a thing may be said to be 'the same'
or 'other' do not alter the fact that in every such case
participation in Sameness or Otherness is involved. Thus
an object *a* partaking of Sameness in relation to *x* might
be regarded as partaking of the same Form and mani-
festing the same quality as *b*, which partakes of Sameness
in relation to *y*; and the same would apply to things that
were other than *x* or other than *y*. We shall presently find
evidence that difference-from-beauty and the like seem
to be treated in this dialogue, and may have been regarded
by Plato, as species of Otherness.[1] If this was Plato's
view, the point that Peck raises would certainly present
no difficulty so far as the present argument is concerned.
It may be added that in the *Phaedo* (74c) he treats Equality
as a Form, although we might regard 'equal' as an
incomplete predicate unless a relationship is expressed
or at least implied.[2] There is no good ground for supposing that in Plato's view 'same' and 'other' could not
be treated as common attributes.

Secondly, it may be noted that at 255b5 (the final
remark of the passage under discussion) the 'is' is clearly
the 'is' of identity; and hence, despite the no doubt
deliberately paradoxical nature of 255a4–5 ('Change and
Rest are neither Other nor the Same'), the 'are' there
should obviously be taken in the same way.

Argument 3: 255b8–c6. The EV next argues that Being and
Sameness are not identical. 'If', he says, 'Being and

---

[1] See p. 166 f.

[2] μέγεθος ('size' or 'tallness') is perhaps another example, since although things can have size apart from their relation to the size of other
things, Plato nowhere says this, and clearly treats the term as relative at
Phaedo 102c-d.

Sameness have no difference in meaning, when we say
that Change and Rest *are*, we shall thereby be speaking
of them as being the same (ταὐτὸν ὡς ὄντα).'

This looks like an argument based upon meaning and
effected by substitution, such as we had at 250a–b. 'Is
the same' is not always interchangeable with a mere 'is'.
But there is a slight difficulty.

Peck objects[1] that when the EV says 'we shall be speaking of them both as being the same', the expression 'the
same' 'is obviously intended to be understood, and is in
fact understood, by Theaetetus to mean "the same *as each
other*" ', and that this is illegitimate. The fact that ταὐτόν
is singular ('as being the same thing') may be thought to
support this view, and it is of course true that the substitution of 'are the same as each other' for 'are' would
not be justified by the hypothesis that Being and Sameness
are identical in meaning. On the other hand, if this is what
the EV is suggesting, his fault is simply that of sub-
stituting a special case of participation in Sameness. His
argument would be valid if he had substituted 'are the
same [as something]', and does not (or need not) depend
on taking a special case. He has already used satisfactorily one argument of simple substitution (250a–b),
and his taking of a particular case here is perhaps to be
attributed simply to a desire to impress Theaetetus. In
the previous argument he has obviously expressed his
demonstrandum and his conclusion in such a way as to
make them sound as paradoxical as possible (255a4–5,
b5–6).

Lacey (49), indeed, maintains that 'the point is that
when we say "Rest and Change are the same", we may
mean that they are the same as each other, but when we

[1] *CQ* 1952, p. 48.

say "Rest and Change are", we do not mean they are each
other'. But although the special case of sameness-with-
each-other could have been used for such an argument,
this meaning is difficult to extract from what the EV says.

We should probably conclude that the EV's wording is
deliberately misleading, but that it is Theaetetus rather
than the reader who is meant to be misled. For Plato the
point will have been the general one, that we cannot substitute 'is the same' for every occurrence of 'is'. Plato
must certainly have regarded the present argument, in one
form or another, as valid, for he goes on to use another
argument to prove that Otherness is distinct from Being,
which could equally well have been used to prove that
Sameness is distinct from Being; and if he believed in the
validity of any of these arguments, he certainly believed
in the validity of this latter one.

Argument 4: 255c8–e1. Taylor translates the argument distinguishing Otherness from Being as follows.

Now shall we name Otherness as a fifth [Form]? Or must we
regard it and Being as a pair of names for one and the same
kind?—It might be so.—Still I conceive you will grant that
some entities are spoken of as absolutes (αὐτὰ καθ' αὐτά),
others always as relative to others (πρὸς ἄλλα).[1] (255c8–13)—
Of course.—And that a thing is only called *other* relatively to
some *other* thing (πρὸς ἕτερον)? (255d1)—Yes.—But this
would not be so if there were not a vast difference in meaning[2] between Being and Otherness. If Otherness, like Being,
participated (μετεῖχε) in both Forms (εἰδοῖν) [i.e. in Moravcsik's terminology, Relationality and Non-relationality: τὸ

---

[1] The manuscript B has πρὸς ἄλληλα (TW have πρὸς ἄλλα).
[2] Literally, just 'a vast difference'. 'In meaning' would be better omitted,
since Forms in a sense are *things meant*: cf. 250b, and p. 147.

πρὸς ἄλλο and τὸ καθ' αὑτό],[1] there would be cases in which an 'other' was *other* without reference to any other thing. But in fact we find it to hold good without qualification that everything which is *other* is what it is—*other*—relatively to something other than itself. (255d3-7)—The facts are as you say.—Thus we must include Otherness as a fifth among our selection of Forms.

Now as Runciman (90) says, Plato surely considered it true to say of any Form that it is (copula) καθ' αὑτό—non-relational—at any rate in a sense.[2] If so, it is impossible to take the EV's meaning in d3-7 to be that the Form Otherness cannot partake of Non-relationality, at least if the Form is regarded as a concept or universal. But neither can θάτερον and τὸ ὄν here be collective terms for the things that partake of Otherness and the things that partake of Being, for all things *are*, and also are other than everything else, so that if anything that 'is' can partake of Non-relationality, anything that 'is other' can do so too. We must therefore rule out both the possibility that in 255d3-7 Plato is thinking of Forms *qua* concepts, and the possibility that he is thinking of things that partake of Otherness and of Being.

(a) Moravcsik's explanation. Moravcsik explains the argument in terms of verbal usage. He has very reasonably

---

[1] These must be the εἴδη meant, though they are never so named. If the term εἴδη elsewhere in this part of the dialogue means Forms, we should probably accept Relationality and Non-relationality as Forms. [Frede (24) rejects attempts to treat the expressions αὐτὰ καθ' αὑτὰ and πρὸς ἄλλα as Forms, for which he sees no evidence anywhere in Plato. He takes them as referring to the modes of being of entities, not to actual properties.]

[2] We are not told in this dialogue that all Forms must be καθ' αὑτά, but it would seem reasonable to suppose that a Form qua concept could still be so described. From earlier works it would appear that even Forms whose instances were relational would themselves be non-relational: cf. *Symp.* 211a-b.

inferred (47) from Argument 3 'the apparent identification
of the Forms Being and the Same with the meanings of
"is" and "is the same" '. He now argues as follows (54):

When Plato says of the Other that it is always relational
(255d1) he does not mean that what partakes of the Other is
always relational, but that instances of " . . . other than . . ."
and thus the meaning of "other" require completion by
another concept in order that we may predicate the Other of
anything. The lines concerning Being should be read to be
likewise about the Form and not about the extension. . . . The
instances of "is" are indeed either relational or non-relational.
The existential "is" does not relate, but the "is" which connects subject and predicate does.

There are several objections to this interpretation.
First there is the difficulty of 255c12–13, which Moravcsik
translates 'of beings we always say that some are relational,
and some non-relational'. The Greek here has τῶν ὄντων,
'of the things that are', i.e. (presumably) 'of the things
that partake of Being'. Moravcsik says that 'the lines
make good sense if we construe Being as including more
than Existence. The instances of "is" are indeed either
relational or non-relational'. But we can hardly take
τῶν ὄντων, to *mean* 'the instances of "is" '; and if it means
'of the things that are' and the 'are' is ambiguous as
between 'have being' and 'are such-and-such', it is still
some of these *things* that are said to be relational, not
some of the instances of 'is'. Again, if Plato was arguing
purely from linguistic usage, we might expect him in
d3–7 to talk not about 'an other' and 'everything that is
other' but about what is *said to be* other.

But the most important consideration is that instances
of the word 'other' and of the copulative 'is' are not
relational in the required sense. The contrast in c12–13 is

clearly a contrast, not of what relates with what does not relate, but of what is related with what is independent and unrelated; and though the existential 'is' might perhaps be described as καθ' αὑτό ('on its own'), the copulative 'is' could not be described as itself πρὸς ἄλλο ('related to something else'). Likewise an instance of ' . . . other than . . . ' relates what precedes to what follows. But the EV suggests in d4–6 that θάτερον (? 'Otherness') is itself πρὸς ἄλλο ('related to something else').

(b) *Suggested solution.* The explanation must be that in d3–7 the EV is talking about the Forms Otherness and Being, but treating them, as he has treated Change and Rest at 252d and in Arguments 1 and 2 above, as paradeigmatic standards. If Otherness is a Form, instances of otherness will be qualities 'in us' in the same way as instances of beauty or tallness may be 'in us' (*Phaedo* 102d–103b). Instances of Otherness are necessarily relational, and hence Otherness itself, *qua* paradeigmatic standard, is necessarily relational and not non-relational. The instances of Being, on the other hand—and hence Being itself *qua* paradeigmatic standard—are not necessarily relational.[1] Therefore Otherness must be distinct from Being.

[1] [Bluck's interpretation, like Plato's text, perhaps fails to explore adequately the precise nature of this duality in Being, presented apparently by both as an established fact. Bluck's next paragraph certainly suggests that he was thinking of the distinction between relational and non-relational characteristics or their standard instances, e.g. Man and Servant. But in a passage of his original manuscript which I have omitted because as it stood it did not square with this view, he indicated awareness of a problem in that this interpretation failed to treat Being and Difference in strictly parallel fashion. 'We might say', he wrote, 'that what is other cannot be non-relational *in respect of its participation in Otherness*; but then it is not true to say that "what is" is both relational and non-relational (or relational in some cases, non-relational in others) *in respect of its participation in Being*.' It is Frede's insistence at several points in his discussion of

It might be objected that Being is treated as partaking of *both* Relationality *and* Non-relationality, but that we cannot be meant to suppose that the standard instance of Being, and hence all instances of Being, will be both relational and non-relational; for while any Form might be described as καθ' αὑτό (non-relational) in a sense, but as πρὸς ἄλλο (relational) as being other than other Forms, it is clear from 255c12–13 that the EV is thinking of things as being *by nature* relational or non-relational. Thus he might say that Man was non-relational, but Servant (vis-à-vis Master) relational. He cannot mean that the standard instance of Being is *both*. Indeed Otherness itself is *ex hypothesi* not non-relational, but would presumably count as an instance of Being. But close inspection shows that the EV is not suggesting that τὸ ὄν (Being) partakes simultaneously of Relationality and of Non-relationality. He says that if θάτερον (Otherness) partook of both, 'there would be cases' in which an instance of it was non-relational; translated literally, what he says is that 'sometimes there would even be one of the things that are other that was other without reference to some-

the passage (12 ff.) on preserving precise parallelism between Being and Otherness that leads him eventually, and on grounds largely similar to Bluck's in other respects too, to interpret the dual aspect of 'what is' as the basic Platonic distinction between Forms and particulars. As an exposition of 255c12–13 and leaving aside the larger structure which Frede erects on it, this is entirely consistent with Bluck's general line of reasoning. The reason why Bluck stopped short of the logical conclusion of his arguments, however, is perhaps that he was reluctant to saddle Plato with so tortuous and unlikely a method of proving Otherness and Being to be separate Kinds. There must surely have been more straight-forward ways of achieving this than to argue from a characteristic which lines Otherness up with the world of particulars as opposed to the Forms. I would in the circumstances agree with Bluck's implied choice: it is better to sacrifice precise parallelism in favour of a more obvious recon-struction of the argument. The distinction between relational and non-relational characteristics is equally basic, and in addition clearly relevant to the nature of Otherness.]

thing else'. Hence, when he suggests that Being partakes of both, what he means is that sometimes we will find an instance that is relational, but that sometimes we will find one that is non-relational.

He has not perhaps expressed himself with precision, but that this must be his meaning is confirmed by c12–13, where some at least of the 'things that are' are treated as being either relational or non-relational, but not as both. Lines d4–6 will mean that if the typical instance of Otherness, like the typical instance of Being, could partake of *either* Form (Relationality or Non-relationality), then there would be cases where an instance of Otherness was non-relational.[1]

There would be no imprecision if we could take θάτερον and τὸ ὄν as collective expressions denoting 'what is other' and 'what is', but this is ruled out, as we have seen, by the fact that if a thing that is partakes of Non-relationality, then so does a thing that is other: for a thing that is will always be a thing that is other than other things. It seems clear, moreover, that τὸ θάτερον in d3 must be the Form Otherness, and in that case it is likely that θάτερον in d4 will also be the Form. The imprecision, such as it is, does not affect the validity of the argument.

2. IDENTIFICATION AND PREDICATION CONTRASTED

The separate identity of the five 'most important Kinds' is now to be regarded as established. There has been no

---

[1] That the EV should say 'both' when he means 'either' is less surprising if we bear in mind that a literal translation would be: 'If the thing that is other, like the thing that is, partook of both. . . .' He is not trying to talk in precise technical language, and the ambiguity of τὸ ὄν could easily account for this slip.

proof of the separateness of Sameness and Otherness, any more than there has been of the separateness of Change and Rest,[1] but presumably the EV would say of the former pair, as he says of the latter (250a), that they are complete opposites, and infer their separateness from that.

The EV now, at 255e, remarks that Otherness pervades all the Forms (εἴδη), 'for each of them is other than the rest not by reason of its own nature, but because it partakes of the Form (ἰδέα) of Otherness'. This reminds us of the puzzlement expressed at 250c–d about Being, which was found to be 'of its own nature' neither changing nor at rest. Since then a good deal of light has been thrown on this puzzle. It has become clear that there is an important difference between predication and identification, and that a thing may have attributes, even necessary and permanent attributes, without their being part of its 'proper nature' or essence. This is the case with Forms that have the attribute of otherness (inasmuch as they are other than *X*, *Y* or *Z*, or all other Forms), and it is also the case with Being, which has the character of being at rest. It has also become clear that the word 'is' is used ambiguously. In 255e–256d the EV removes all possible doubt about these matters in a series of propositions concerning the relationship of Change to the other Forms discussed.

1. (a) Change is not (identical with) Rest   255e11–15
    (b) Change is (by partaking of Being)   256a1

---

[1] Moravcsik (43) writes, apropos the argument at 254d7–12: 'We are told that Motion and Rest must be two separate entities because they do not "mix".' But all that we are in fact told is that Rest, Change and Being must be three separate entities, because Being mixes with the other two whereas they do not mix with each other (see p. 135, n. 2 above).

2. (a) Change is not (identical with) the Same   256a3–5
   (b) Change is the same (by partaking of the Same)
                                                    256a7–8

3. (a) Change is not (identical with) Other   256c5–8
   (b) Change is other (by partaking of Otherness)[1]
                                                    256c5–8

4. (a) Change is not (identical with) Being   256d5–8
   (b) Change is (by partaking of Being)   256d8–9

It will be seen that proposition 1(b) spoils the symmetry
of the four pairs of contrasted statements. Not only does
this proposition not provide the same sort of contrast
with 1(a) as we find in the other three pairs—a contrast
between being identical with, and partaking of, one
particular Form—but its presence here is unnecessary,
for it appears again as 4(b). This arrangement is probably
deliberate. It looks as though the EV—and Plato—is
disinclined, in what is to some extent a résumé of results
already reached, to assert as true what has hitherto been
assumed to be impossible—that Change rests (by partaking
of Rest). But after putting forward the second pair of
propositions, and before putting forward the third, the EV
asks (256b6–7), 'Then even if Change itself participated
in some way in Rest, there would be nothing at all
absurd in speaking of it as "at rest"?' This inserted
question seems intended to suggest that there must, in
fact, be a sense in which Change participates in Rest.[2] This

---

[1] The word μετέχειν ('partake') is not used in this instance, for the
EV prefers to play on the verbal paradox that since 'Change is other than
the Other', it is 'not Other in a way, and yet also other'.

[2] [But not, surely, the sense which Crombie suggests (vol. II, p. 400;
cf. p. 398, 406) of stable or uniform activity, which it would be very
forced indeed to call 'stationary' or 'resting'. Wiehl's reference (199)
to *Theaetetus* 182c ff. is also misleading.]

would of course have to be a sense which did not involve
identification and therefore the reversal of the 'proper
nature' of Change; but that is involved, as we have seen,
only if Change is regarded as itself a paradeigmatic
instance of change. It is impossible to be sure whether
Plato himself appreciated this fact or not, but probably,
as no explanation of this important point is offered, he
was himself somewhat puzzled.[1]

3. CONCLUSION

The purpose of this section has been to investigate the
natures of certain important Kinds, and their power of
having communion with one another. The separate
identity of the Kinds selected (including Being) is proved,
and the distinction between identification and predication
is finally established: and we thus find that a 'thing that is'
can have a nature of its own and *be*, not by being identical
with Being or with anything else, but by partaking of
Being. This will help to explain the nature of an image,[2]
for the 'being' of an image is not disproved by showing
that it *is not* the original; all that is necessary for it to be is
that it should itself partake of Being. At the same time
the discussion of 'what is' has helped to throw light on
'what is not', as the EV hoped that it would (250e-251a),[3]
by suggesting that a 'thing that is not' may also have a
nature of its own and 'be' by partaking of Being, and yet
'not be' in the sense that it is *not identical* with something.

It is already implicit in 255e ff. that non-identity is to be
accounted for by participation in Otherness, and this is
presently made explicit (256d-e).

[1] See also p. 114 f.   [2] Cf. p. 65 f.   [3] See p. 106.

APPENDIX

The Greek of 255a10–b1 is this:

κίνησίς τε στήσεται καὶ στάσις αὖ κινηθήσεται· περὶ γὰρ
ἀμφότερα θάτερον ὁποτερονοῦν γιγνόμενον αὐτοῖν ἀναγκάσει
μεταβάλλειν αὖ θάτερον ἐπὶ τοὐναντίον τῆς αὐτοῦ φύσεως,
ἅτε μετασχὸν τοῦ ἐναντίου.

The rendering given in the text (version 1) involves the
idea that although e.g. Change will have become Rest,
if Rest can be attributed to it, yet Rest must also reverse its
own nature. The argument must be that if Change becomes Rest in this way, it will then also be identifiable
with the mutual attribute (e.g. Otherness) with which
Rest is *ex hypothesi* identical. Change will therefore be an
attribute of Rest, and so cause the second reversal of
nature.

[Bluck's interpretation involves something of the confusion between identity and predication which he objects
to when discussing Runciman's explanation in 2 (*b*) above.
He makes Plato jump from the premiss 'Change has the
attribute Rest' to the conclusion 'Change is identical with
Rest', justifying this in 2(*c*) on the basis of the paradigm-
case aspect of the Forms. I accept that for entities of this
sort, as far as their 'proper natures' are concerned, a
reversal of nature is involved if their contraries are to be
predicable of them. This is also implied by version 2 and
by Taylor's translation (version 3 below).

But not even essential predication amounts to identity.
In any case, the separateness of Change and Rest has been
so fundamental an assumption throughout the dialogue
(see, for example, Argument 1 above) that it seems
highly unlikely that Plato would now hazard an argument

that involves denying it. And what sense could we give to the passage 255a11–b1, if, as Bluck believes, this stage of the argument *starts* from the identity of Change and Rest? If $X=Y$, what price a tortuous proof that Y must also 'turn into' X? For these reasons I prefer Cornford's interpretation, which is followed too by Wiehl; see also below. Ed.]

Cornford's translation (version 2: see text) takes περὶ ἀμφότερα γιγνόμενον together (so too Dies). This seems legitimate in spite of Moravcsik's doubts (46, n. 1), though the form of expression is not found elsewhere. But Cornford ignores the αὖ in a12, which seems to echo the αὖ in a10 and to indicate that the second reversal of nature is being treated as an additional paradox which follows from the first.

[This is a difficulty. As Moravcsik (46) puts it, 'the text contains a conjunction, and the "καὶ . . . . αὖ . . ." construction cannot be taken as a disjunctive'. However, in view of the rather more compelling problems which I have indicated above with regard to Bluck's interpretation, I would prefer to assume a certain looseness in Plato's language. This can perhaps be justified on some such grounds as Berger (75) adduces. Ed.]

Taylor seems to be trying to explain the second reversal of nature when he translates (version 3): 'For if either of them be present in both, it will compel the other, in its turn, to assume the character of its contrary, in virtue of its participation in contrariety.' But if we are to suppose that (e.g.) Rest, although reversing the nature of Change by being predicated of it, will also force Change to turn into the character of the contrary of Rest (viz. Change itself), it is odd that the former effect receives (in this version) no mention at all, and also that the expression 'turn into' (μεταβάλλειν) should have been used. The latter difficulty is perhaps explained by a footnote which suggests (though it is difficult to obtain the required sense from his translation), that he had in mind an interpretation similar to Lacey's (49): if (e.g.) Rest is identified with the Other, and so changes the nature of Change by being predicated of it, Change, as being the contrary of Rest, must be identical with the Same, the contrary of Other, and therefore predicable of Rest—so that the nature of Rest is also reversed. This meaning would in fact be better given by version 1, if instead of saying 'through having come to partake of its opposite' we say 'because it partakes of contrariety'.

However, neither Taylor nor Lacey give any particular importance to the tense of the participle (μετασχόν). The aorist here suggests strongly that the reference is not to the established and unquestioned relationship of contrariety between Change and Rest (or Same and Other) but rather to something which arises *ex hypothesi* in this particular argument. In any case on Lacey's interpretation too much is left to be inferred.

THE REINSTATEMENT OF 'WHAT IS NOT'

1. THE BEING AND NOT-BEING OF THE KINDS

Having reached the conclusion that Change is 'a thing that is not' (οὐκ ὄν), because it is not Being, and also that it is 'a thing that is' (ὄν), because it partakes of Being, the EV continues (256d–e):

It must then be possible for 'that which is not' (*or* 'the thing that is not', τὸ μὴ ὄν) to *be*, not only in the case of Change but so far as *all* the Kinds are concerned. For throughout all of them the nature of Otherness so operates as to make each one of them other than Being (τὸ ὄν),[1] and so 'a thing that is not' (οὐκ ὄν), and in the same way we shall be right in saying of all alike that they are 'things that are not' (οὐκ ὄντα), and again, because they partake of Being (τὸ ὄν), that they 'are' and are 'things that are' (εἶναί τε καὶ ὄντα). . . . In the case, then, of each one of the Forms, πολὺ μέν ἐστι τὸ ὄν, ἄπειρον δὲ πλήθει τὸ μὴ ὄν.

Cornford translates these last words, 'there is much that it *is* and an indefinite number of things that it *is not*', and this is probably the correct sense. It might perhaps seem strange to infer from the fact that every Kind partakes of Being that there is 'much' that it is, and from the

---

[1] This was the meaning of τοῦ ὄντος in 256d ('Change is other than Being'), and is therefore almost certainly its meaning here, even though 'what is (so-and-so)' would make good sense.
[It is hard to see how Owen (233, n. 20) can justify his view that 'being' (τὸ ὄν) in this passage is not the name of an abstract entity but simply a predicate. How could it make sense for the EV to claim that 'we shall be right in saying of all alike . . . because they possess the predicate "being" (τοῦ ὄντος) that they . . . are "things that are" (ὄντα)'?]

fact that each is distinct from Being that it is likely to be
distinct from an indefinite number of things. The more
natural inference might seem rather that many things will
probably partake not only of Being but of each of the
other Forms as well, and that whereas all Kinds alike
'are not' Being, similarly in all probability an indefinite
number of things will 'not be' each of the Kinds: 'in the
case of each of the Forms there is much that is (partakes
of) that Form, and again *what is not that Form* will be unlimited in number'. On the other hand, to make it possible
to obtain this sense from the text, the first sentence of the
passage quoted would have to mean that in the case of each
of the Kinds there exists 'that which is not *that Kind*'.[1] But
from the following sentence it is clear that it is Change and
each of the other Kinds that are thought of as being
'things that are not'—the *subjects* in statements denying
their identity with Being—and 'that which is not' in the
first sentence quoted is therefore almost certainly intended to be a description of the subject of any such
statement.

The meaning then will be this. Each Kind is distinct
from Being and so is a 'thing that is not' and yet partakes
of Being and so is a 'thing that is';[2] and in fact it seems
that in the case of each Form its 'being' is plentiful and its
'not-being' unlimited in number—it 'is' many things and
it 'is not' an unlimited number of things.[3] This last

[1] [For a different attempt to find the missing premiss in the text see
Owen (233, n. 21).]

[2] As Runciman (85) points out, μετέχει τοῦ ὄντος in 256e3 cannot, as
Ackrill (1) and Cornford (288) suggest, correspond to any exclusively
existential sense of εἶναι. That is ruled out by 256e5–6. [See now Owen,
253 ff.]

[3] [The awkwardness of Cornford's translation of 256e5 f., which
involves taking τὸ ὄν in the highly dubious sense of 'that which *it* is' and
τὸ μὴ ὄν as 'that which *it* is not', is avoided by Frede's hypothesis of an
'inverted' use of ἔστιν (52 ff.) He suggests that both here and earlier at

observation will be an inference not simply from the fact that each Form is and is not Being, but also, we may suppose, from what was said a little earlier about Change being and yet not being 'the same' and 'other'; for that, too, must be true of all Forms. There will of course be many other things also that each Form 'is not'.

2. THE NOT-BEING OF 'WHAT IS'

The EV now takes the particular case of Being (257a).

Being itself also must be said to be other than the rest. . . . Being, too, it seems, 'is not' in as many ways as there are other things. For not being those things, it is its single self, but it is not the other things, which are unlimited in number.

Fowler translates 'not being those things, it is itself one, and again, those other things are not unlimited in number'. But this contradicts the previous statement (256e) that there is an unlimited number of things that each Form is not. Fowler remarks, 'not only is it true that every thing in each of the classes is not, but not-being extends also to all conceptions which do not and cannot have any reality'. But 'unlimited number' need mean no more than 'an extremely large number'; and nothing need be included apart from the other Forms. (The ἕν loses its point unless there is a contrast between the *one* thing that Being is, and the *unlimited number* of things that it is not.)

256d11 to say 'τὸ μὴ ὄν (or τὸ ὄν) is in respect of *X*' is an alternative way of saying '*X* is οὐκ ὄν (or ὄν)'. The substance of Bluck's interpretation is not affected: Plato must still be discussing what (e.g.) Change is and is not, not what is (partakes of) and is not (identical with) Change. But the first sentence he translates (256d11 f.) will now read: 'It must therefore be possible for Not-being to be not only in respect of Change, but also of all the Kinds.' 256e5 f. would mean: 'That which is in respect of each of the Forms, then, is considerable, and that which is not in respect of each is unlimited'.]

Now at 241d the EV made it clear that he proposed to refute Parmenides' pronouncement and prove 'that what is not, in some respect is, and that what is, in a way is not'. Since in what follows the present passage (257b–258c) he offers further argument to show that it is possible for 'what is not' to 'be' but says nothing about the converse proposition, it would seem reasonable to suppose, as Cornford (289) does, that we are concerned with that converse here.

Yet it is difficult to believe that τὸ ὄν means 'what is' here. Its meaning throughout this passage has been 'Being':[1] that is what τοῦ ὄντος meant at 256d (the Kind Change 'is not' the Kind Being), and must therefore have meant it again at 256e3. It can hardly refer to anything but the Form now (n.b. the use of αὐτό, 'itself'). Cornford simply says that 'τὸ ὄν here . . . is verbally ambiguous', but apart from making the argument unnecessarily captious, this scarcely solves the problem; for the natural way to take the expression here would be as referring, unambiguously, to the Form.

The problem is solved, however, if we suppose that the Form Being is again being treated, as we saw that it was in 255c–d (and as Change and Rest have several times been treated),[2] as a paradeigmatic standard. If the standard Thing-that-is can 'not be', then this must be true of any instance of Being, and Parmenides is indeed rebutted on this point. 'We must not', says the EV (257a), 'be disturbed even by this conclusion [that Being or the Thing-that-is can "not be"], if the nature of the Kinds is such that they have communion with one another.'

---

[1] Even if it should be taken at 256e1 in the rather special sense of 'what is so-and-so' (see p. 157 n.), that sense could not apply here.

[2] See p. 142. Cf. p. 113 ff.

3. THE BEING OF 'WHAT IS NOT'

'Let us consider this next point also,' says the EV (257b), and follows this remark by offering an extended argument which has to a considerable extent defied interpretation. It is clearly a further attempt, and one crucial for the dialogue as a whole, to vindicate the 'ontological respectability' of 'what is not', as its conclusion at 258bc indicates. But it is by no means clear exactly what meaning we are to give to 'what is not' in this particular argument. The grand summary of the case against Parmenides which Plato gives at 258c–259d (particularly 258d5–e3) might suggest that the present passage is to be regarded as an advance on the stage reached at 256d–e: there the EV had demonstrated the Being of 'what is not', now apparently he offers a definition of its essential nature or 'Form' (εἶδος) as well. But it is doubtful that Plato really intended to convey the impression that 257b–258c was dealing with the same problem of negative identity which he has been concerned with earlier.

The argument begins (257b3): 'When we say "that which is not" (τὸ μὴ ὄν), we do not, it seems, mean something opposed to "that which is" (τοῦ ὄντος), but only something that is other [than that].' It would be possible to understand the EV here as saying 'we do not mean something opposed to Being, but something that is other than Being', and this would have to be an allusion to the possibility mentioned above (section 1) of describing as 'a thing that is not' the subject of a statement asserting the non-identity of the subject with Being. But the examples that follow[1] lead us to think not

---

[1] [Owen claims (232) that what follows is not example but analogy, though 'it is often tacitly denied'. It is true that Bluck does not explicitly

of statements of non-identity, but of negative predication. Plato now appears to be concerned with something much more general than non-identity with Being;
it would in any case be odd to revert here to statements
with that particular predicate.

It seems better, therefore, to assume that 'that which is
not' means 'that what is not (copula) X' and 'that which
is' means 'that which is (copula) X'. The point will then
be that when we talk about 'that which is not' in allusion
to something that is not X, we do not necessarily mean
something that is characterized by the opposite of X,
but only something that does not possess the character
of X-ness. This is made clear by the illustration (257bc).

For instance, when we speak of something as not large, may
we not just as well mean by the expression what is *equal* as
what is *small*? . . . When it is said that a negative signifies an
opposite, we shall not agree, but only allow that the use of
'not' indicates something different from the words that follow
—or rather from the things denoted by the words that follow
the negative.[1]

The immediate point therefore is not, as Cornford (289)
supposes it is, 'that "that which is not" in this sense is
distinct from "Non-existence" and from "the non-

refute the analogy interpretation, or consider the evidence for 'the
familiar Greek idea of a middle state between contraries as containing
something of both extremes', which Owen cites (235) to make this
interpretation possible. But of the latter there is no hint here, and as
Owen stresses that 'is' and 'is not' in the *Sophist* are always two-place
predicates requiring completion by some other term (e.g. large), it is
hard not to regard any particular completion (e.g. x is not large) as an
illustration or example of the use of ' . . . is not'.]

[1] [Owen rightly points out (238) that most translations may mislead
Greekless readers because in translation the fact is usually concealed that
Greek, unlike English, makes the verb 'to be' follow the negative in
expressions like τὸ μὴ ὄν ('what is not') and generally in negative pre-
dications with οὐκ ἔστιν ('is not'). This is a caution which Bluck would
no doubt heartily endorse.]

existent" '—or even from 'that which has no being'. That
is indeed the lesson of this part of the dialogue as a
whole.[1] But for the moment we are concerned with the
more general implication of negatively predicating *any*
property of a subject.

It has often been held that what Plato has in mind is a
range of incompatibles: that when we say 'that which is
not [*X*]' we mean 'that which is incompatible [with *X*]'.
Those who hold this view appeal to the illustration, and
to the fact that if a thing is equal to something it cannot
also be large in comparison with the same thing. They
explain any obscurity of expression by pointing out that
Plato lacked any technical term with which to express
the notion of incompatibility.[2] However, precisely because of Plato's lack of a technical vocabulary one might
have expected him to make his point clear in ordinary
language, had his meaning been what is alleged. Taking
ἕτερον to mean 'incompatible', which probably springs
from a desire to find reference to incompatibles in the
passage explaining false statement, is in any case quite
unnecessary. Both passages make good sense if the EV is
here taken to be saying that 'that which is not' can mean
'that which is other'.

The EV now proceeds to the next stage of the argument:

The nature of Otherness is, like knowledge, cut up into
pieces. . . . Knowledge, like Otherness, is one, but each part
of it that has to do with a particular subject is marked off and
has a name of its own; and hence we talk about many arts and
many kinds of knowledge (257c7–d2). . . . This same thing is

[1] See p. 160.
[2] Cf. Hamlyn, 292. For the case against this view, see also Moravcsik,
67 ff.

true of the parts of the nature of Otherness, although that nature is one. . . . Is there a part of the Other that is set in contrast to the Beautiful? (257d4–7). . . . Shall we say that this is nameless, or shall we say that it has a special name? (257d9)

Theaetetus replies that it has a special name: 'what on any occasion we refer to as "not beautiful", this is what is other than the nature of the Beautiful'. (257d10–11). The EV continues:

Being marked off [as part of] a single Kind of the things that are and again set in contrast with one of the things that are, this surely constitutes the being of 'the Not-beautiful' (τὸ μὴ καλόν)? . . . So 'the Not-beautiful' turns out, it seems, to be the setting of something that is in contrast with something that is (257e2–7). . . . Well, according to this argument do we find that 'the Not-beautiful' has any less right than the Beautiful to be counted among the things that are? (257e9–10). . . . Then 'the Not-large' and the Large itself must be said equally to be? . . . And we must also put 'the Not-just' on the same footing as the Just, inasmuch as the one 'is' no less than the other? . . . And we shall say the same of all the rest, since the nature of Otherness has been shown to be among the things that are, and if that is so, we must count its parts also as things that are, just as much as anything else (258a). . . . So, it seems, the setting of a part of the nature of the Other and [a part][1] of the nature of Being side by side in contrast with one another is, if one may say so, as much something that is (οὐσία) as Being itself. It does not signify something opposed to that [i.e. to that part of the nature of Being], but only something that is other than that. . . . What then are we to call it? (258a11–b5)

Theaetetus replies, 'Clearly this is just the "what-is-not"

---

[1] If we do not supply μορίου with Campbell here from the previous line, we shall have to interpret the passage as referring back to non-identity with Being, which would raise the same problems as at 257b above.

that we were looking for because of the Sophist', and the EV goes on:

> Has it then, as you say, no less being than anything else? And may we now confidently assert that 'that which is not' assuredly *is*, having its own nature—as the Large was large and the Beautiful was beautiful, so too with 'the Not-large' and 'the Not-beautiful'—and so too 'that which is not' in the same way both was and is a 'thing that is not', a single Form to be counted among the many things that are? (258b–c)

The main question here is what is meant by 'the Not-beautiful' and so on. Cornford (293) took 'the Not-beautiful' to be 'a collective name for all the Forms there are, other than the Beautiful itself', and hence has to suppose (293 f.), when it is said to be a part of the Different (the Other), that 'the Different must mean "that which is different". Since every part of the field of Forms is different from every other part, the whole field can be called "the Different" .' But it would appear to be a part of the *nature* of the Other (258a), and if Forms are to be found anywhere in the *Sophist*, this 'nature' ought to be one of them.[1]

Moreover, the Not-beautiful can hardly be just 'any instance of Difference from Beauty'. At 257e9–10 the EV 'can hardly mean that anything that is not Beauty is as real or existent as Beauty unless he will also maintain that nothing is less real or existent than Beauty; for everything except Beauty itself, however unreal it may be, is different from Beauty' (Runciman, 101).

Peck (*CQ* 1952, 52) takes the description of the nature

[1] [Kamlah (43) and Wiggins (292) also seem to overlook the role of the Other as an independent Form. '*x* is not large' is not understood by Plato, as they suggest, as equivalent to '*x* partakes of some Form other than Largeness', but rather as '*x* partakes of Difference from Largeness (the Large)'.]

of Otherness as 'cut up into pieces' as one argument
against regarding it as a Form.[1] 'A "Form" which is
chopped up into pieces is a strange candidate for the
status of a Platonic Form. We are bound to infer that
such a "Form" has no proper nature or unity at all.' But
the EV indicates what he has in mind by means of the
analogy of knowledge. Knowledge is a generic term, of
which there are many species: the EV talks of 'each part
(μέρος) of it that has to do with a particular subject'
being marked off by its own name. There is no reason to
suppose that Plato would deny that Knowledge was a
Form, and therefore no reason either to draw any such
conclusion in respect of Otherness.

Now the EV talks about the Not-beautiful and the
Not-large and so on as 'parts' of the nature of Otherness.
The terms for 'part' (μόριον and μέρος) are often used to
mean 'species', and we find that the 'parts' of Otherness
are analogous to the 'parts' of knowledge, each of which
is applied to some special field. It is natural, therefore,
to take the EV's question at 257d as to whether there is a
part of the Other set in contrast to the Beautiful to be
concerned with a possible species of Otherness (Difference), namely, Difference-from-Beauty. This will be a
quality that contrasts with the quality of Beauty; or, if
we are to talk in terms of paradeigmatic standards—for
whether this is itself a Form or not, we must suppose
that Otherness is—it will be the standard 'Thing-that-is-
not-beautiful' contrasted with the Beautiful. Theaetetus'
reply at 257d is in terms of concrete instances, but that is
not surprising in a respondent in a Platonic dialogue.
When the EV goes on to suggest in 257e that the Not-
beautiful is 'marked off from a single Kind', this will

---

[1] Other arguments of Peck's on this point are discussed on pp. 120, 142f.

mean that as each part (species) of knowledge is marked
off from the genus knowledge (257c–d), so the Not-
beautiful (Difference-from-Beauty) is marked off from
the genus Difference.[1]

'The setting of something that is in contrast with something that is' (257e) will mean the setting, not of any non-
beautiful Form in contrast with the Beautiful, but of a
particular species of Otherness, the Not-beautiful (the
Thing-that-is-other-than-beautiful), in contrast with the
Beautiful. This is shown by comparison with 257d7 and
258a11–b1. That this 'setting in contrast' should itself be
equated with the Not-beautiful may appear illogical, but
a less literal and nevertheless legitimate rendering here
might be, ' "the Not-beautiful" turns out to be something that is which is contrasted with something that is'.

If the Not-beautiful is not simply any or all of the
Forms that may be described as other than beautiful, but
a species of Otherness, the question arises whether the
status accorded to it of being a 'thing that is' means
that it is a Form in its own right.[2] It seems in fact that
Plato did not regard negative expressions such as not-
human or not-Greek as corresponding to Forms that
could be subdivided (*Statesman* 262b ff.; cf. *Phaedrus* 265e).
This is not of course proof that they are not Forms, only
that they are of no use in Division. But it does lend some
support to the view that we should not be thinking in
terms of Forms for negative qualities here. But if the
Not-beautiful is a species of Otherness but not itself a

[1] [Crombie's interpretation (vol. II, p. 409) is ingenious, but surely
unduly influenced by the logical distinction between class and property.
He seems to me first to have read the distinction into the passage, and
then to be using the passage as evidence for its occurrence in Plato.]
[2] See Peck, *Phronesis* (1962), 64: 'If τὸ καλόν here is a Platonic Form,
the text gives us no warrant for refusing the same title to τὸ μὴ καλόν.'
Peck's solution, however, is to take *neither* as Forms in this context.

Form, two further questions arise which require investigation. (i) Can we still maintain that the Beautiful, with which it is contrasted, is (for Plato) a Form? (ii) Is there evidence here that Plato has abandoned his gradational ontology?

The EV has said (257e) that the being of the Not-beautiful is derived from the fact that it is marked off from a thing that is (Otherness) and set in contrast with a thing that is (Beauty), and a little later on he remarks (258a) that the parts of Otherness must be things that are since the nature of Otherness has been found to be one. It seems possible that Difference-from-Beauty, even if not a separate Form on its own, might be regarded as a thing that is because Difference (Otherness) is a Form and Beauty is a Form. In that case negative expressions, Not-beautiful, Not-just, etc., would not need to denote separate Forms because they would already each refer to two Forms. Since it is always rash to press Plato's analogies beyond their expressed purpose, there is no need to assume that if there are Forms of particular branches of knowledge, there must also be Forms corresponding to the 'parts' of Difference.

The puzzling phraseology about the 'setting in contrast' of two things that are might suggest that Plato has in mind something more complex than a straightforward Form, because it would have been simpler, if the Not-beautiful were meant to be a Form, to prove its status as a thing that is from its relation to the *one* Form Difference. The complicated explanation of its relation to the *two* Forms Difference and Beauty could then be interpreted as indicating that 'the Not-beautiful' is a shorthand expression referring basically to the Form Difference, but because this is a relational idea, also including a reference to the Form in relation to which the Not-beautiful is different. There would not need to be separate Forms for all negative expressions: this one Form (Difference or Otherness) would account for all such negatives and enable us correctly to assert that something *really is not* such-and-such. On this interpretation there is no difficulty about Beauty itself being a Form: that indeed is a prerequisite of the argument about the 'setting in contrast' of two Forms. Nor need there be any fear that Plato must have abandoned his gradational ontology. The Not-beautiful, even if not a separate Form, need not be interpreted as concrete instance: it would simply be Difference (or the Thing-that-is-different) in a particular application or relation.

However, this interpretation must remain speculative, and has the disadvantage of imputing to Plato explorations into new relationships among Forms (and also between Forms and language) which he never developed. Provided the dislike for negative expressions indicated in the *Statesman* is not thought to prevent it,[1] the Not-beautiful and other negative qualities may more easily be taken as Forms here, though not as Forms which can be used in Collection and Division.

If the Not-beautiful is a Form, it is of course as much a 'thing that is' as the nature of the Beautiful with which it is contrasted. The Not-large and the Not-just and all other species of Difference will likewise be 'things that are'. In fact, what is contrasted with any 'part' or species of Being—that is to say, with any Form, since all Forms are species of Being—will be as much a 'thing that is'

---

[1] [Frede (92 ff.) also argues for the existence of negative Forms in the *Sophist,* and suggests that the limitation imposed in the *Statesman* is a later development in Plato's thinking.]

as is Being itself (258a–b). 'The Not-X' does not necessarily denote a nature that is the opposite of X-ness, but
only one that is other than X-ness (258b).

On either of these interpretations of particular negative
qualities, 'that which is not' itself must be a Form 'with
a nature of its own' (258bc). It is the generic Form of
Otherness (Difference). But this result is in fact no
advance on the stage reached at 256e. The claim at 258d ff.
to have achieved even more than was necessary for the
refutation of Parmenides is still justified, but the success
in establishing the nature of Not-being can no longer
be located solely in this final argument (257b–258c).[1]
It had already been achieved with the analysis of 'is not'
in terms of the Other in the discussion of the inter-
relationships of the Kinds.

What particular purpose, then, is served by this section? There is no longer any reason to doubt that Plato's
intention was to apply the analysis of 'what is not', which
had previously been explored only in the context of non-
identity, to the realm of negative predication as well. He
may well have seen this as a more complex problem
which, if not solved, could be used to cast doubt on his
claims to have laid the bogey of Not-being. Hence his
concern to show that here too the identification with
Otherness holds good.

There is, therefore, no justification for Runciman's
contention (101) that Plato 'makes no distinction between
negative identity and negative predication'. The fact
that the argument about such things as 'that which is not
beautiful' is treated as completely separate from the
argument about 'things that are not Being' is surely proof
that he did draw precisely that distinction. Certainly both

[1] See p. 161.

are subsumed under the Form of 'the Other', but that is no reason in itself for accusing Plato of totally confusing the two things.

Once again the explanation can be found in the conception of the Forms as paradigm cases (for references see p. 113, n. 2). The standard Thing-that-is-other will be totally other, that is to say both quantitatively and qualitatively distinguishable from whatever it is being contrasted with. Of any two Forms that are non-identical with each other (e.g. Rest and Being) it will be true to say, since they are themselves conceived of as standard instances, that of their proper nature they are also qualitatively different. This will apply even where the Forms in question are species of the same genus: e.g. Productive Art and Acquisitive Art will differ in quality as well as identity (so of course will Sitting and Flying; see 263b). And between any two instances of the same Form in the physical world (e.g. between two beds), there will also, owing to the changeability and imperfection of matter, be a substantial element of qualitative difference.

4. CONCLUSION

Having shown that Being and Not-being inhere together in the Kinds, Not-being being analysable in terms of participation in the Other, Plato has proceeded to explain how Being itself in a very extensive sense 'is not'. He has then applied his analysis to the problem of negative attribution, and reached a similar result, without falling into any culpable confusion between identity and predication. The EV's conclusion (258d) is fully justified: 'we have not only shown', as against Parmenides' pronouncements, 'that "things that are not" (τὰ μὴ ὄντα) are, but we have also revealed what the Form (εἶδος) of Not-being (τοῦ μὴ ὄντος) actually is.'

BIBLIOGRAPHY OF WORKS CITED

Books and articles are cited in the text by author's name alone, except where more than one work by an author is discussed in the course of the commentary. Reference should be made to this bibliography for precise identification.

ACKRILL, J. L., 'Plato and the copula: *Sophist* 251–259', *JHS* 77 (1957), 1; reprinted in R. E. Allen (ed.), *Studies* and in G. Vlastos (ed.), *Plato*, vol. 1.

ALLEN, R. E., 'Participation and predication in Plato's middle dialogues', *PR* 69 (1960), 147; reprinted in R. E. Allen (ed.), *Studies*.

ALLEN, R. E. (ed.), *Studies in Plato's Metaphysics*, London, 1965.

BERGER, F. R., 'Rest and motion in the *Sophist*', *Phronesis* 10 (1965), 70.

BIGGER, C. P., *Participation: A Platonic Inquiry*, Louisiana, 1968.

BLUCK, R. S., 'False statement in the *Sophist*', *JHS* 77 (1957), 181.

BLUCK, R. S., 'Forms as Standards', *Phronesis* 2 (1957), 115.

BLUCK, R. S., 'Logos and Forms in Plato: a reply to Professor Cross', *Mind* 65 (1956), 522; reprinted in R. E. Allen (ed.), *Studies*.

BLUCK, R. S., 'Plato's Form of Equal', *Phronesis* 4 (1959), 5.

BLUCK, R. S., *Plato's 'Meno'*, Cambridge, 1961.

BLUCK, R. S., *Plato's 'Phaedo'*, London, 1955.

BLUCK, R. S., 'The *Parmenides* and the "Third Man" ', *CQ* NS 6 (1956), 29.

BOOTH, N. B., 'Plato, *Sophist* 231a, etc.', *CQ* NS 6 (1956), 89.

CAMPBELL, L., *The 'Sophistes' and 'Politicus' of Plato*, Oxford, 1867.

CHERNISS, H., *Aristotle's Criticism of Plato and the Academy*, vol. 1, Baltimore, 1944.

CHERNISS, H., 'The Relation of the *Timaeus* to Plato's later dialogues', *AJP* 78 (1957), 225.

CORNFORD, F. M., *Plato's Theory of Knowledge*, London, 1935.

CROMBIE, I. M., *An Examination of Plato's Doctrines*, vol. II: *Plato on Knowledge and Reality*, London, 1963.

CROSS, R. C., 'Logos and Forms in Plato', *Mind* 63 (1954), 433; reprinted in R. E. Allen (ed.), *Studies*.

, A. (ed.), *Le 'Sophiste'*, *Plato*, vol. 8, Pt. 3, Budé Library, Paris, 1925.

DODDS, E. R. (ed.), Plato, *Gorgias*, Oxford, 1959.

FOWLER, H. N., *'Theaetetus' and 'Sophist'*, *Plato*, vol. 2, Loeb Library, 1942.

FREDE, M., *Prädikation und Existenzaussage*, *Hypomnemata* 18, Göttingen, 1967.

GULLEY, N. C., *Plato's Theory of Knowledge*, London, 1962.

HACKFORTH, R., *Plato's Examination of Pleasure*, Cambridge, 1945.

HAMLYN, D. W., 'The Communion of Forms and the development of Plato's logic', *PQ* 5 (1955), 289.

KAHN, C. H., 'The Greek verb "to be" and the concept of Being', *Foundations of Language* 2 (1966), 1945.

KAHN, C. H., *The Verb 'To Be' in Ancient Greek*, *Foundations of Language* Supplementary Series 16, Pt. 6, Dordrecht, 1973.

KAMLAH, W., *Platons Selbstkritik im 'Sophistes'*, *Zetemata* 33, 1963.

KERFERD, G. B., 'Plato's noble art of sophistry', *CQ* NS 4 (1954), 84.

KOHNKE, F. W., 'Plato's conception of τὸ οὐκ ὄντως οὐκ ὄν', *Phronesis* 2 (1957), 32.

LACEY, A. R., 'Plato's *Sophist* and the Forms', *CQ* NS 9 (1959), 43.

MALCOLM, J., 'Plato's analysis of τὸ ὄν and τὸ μὴ ὄν in the *Sophist*', *Phronesis* 12 (1967), 130.

MARTEN, R., *Der Logos der Dialektik*, Berlin, 1965.

MEINHARDT, H., *Teilhabe bei Platon*, Freiburg/Munich, 1968.

MILLS, K. W., 'Plato's *Phaedo* 74b7–c6, part 2', *Phronesis* 3 (1958), 40.

MORAVCSIK, J. M. E., 'Being and meaning in the *Sophist*', *Acta Philosophica Fennica* 14 (1962), 23.

OWEN, G. E. L., 'Plato on Not-being', in G. Vlastos (ed.), *Plato*, vol. 1, 1971.

PECK, A. L., 'Plato and the μέγιστα γένη of the *Sophist*: a reinterpretation', *CQ* NS 2 (1952), 32.

PECK, A. L., 'Plato's *Sophist*: the συμπλοκὴ τῶν εἰδῶν', *Phronesis* 7 (1962), 46.

ROBINSON, R., *Plato's Earlier Dialectic*, New York, 1941.

ROSS, W. D., *Plato's Theory of Ideas*, Oxford, 1951.

RUNCIMAN, W. G., *Plato's Later Epistemology*, Cambridge, 1962.

SAYRE, K. M., *Plato's Analytic Method*, Chicago, 1969.

SCHIPPER, E. W., 'The meaning of Existence in Plato's *Sophist*', *Phronesis* 9 (1964), 38.

SKEMP, J. B., *Plato's Statesman*, London, 1952.

SOUILHÉ, J., *Étude sur le terme* Δύναμις *dans les dialogues de Platon*, Paris, 1919.

TAYLOR, A. E., *Plato, the Man and his Work*, London, 1926 (referred to in the text as Taylor, *Plato*).

TAYLOR, A. E., *Plato, The Sophist and the Statesman*, London, 1961 (referred to in the text as Taylor, without further specification).

TREVASKIS, J. R., 'The sophistry of noble lineage', *Phronesis* 1 (1955), 36.

VLASTOS, G. (ed.), *Plato,* vol. 1: *Metaphysics and Epistemology*, New York, 1971.

WIEHL, R., *Platon: Der 'Sophist'* (Apelt's German translation revised and annotated), Hamburg, 1967.

WIGGINS, D., 'Sentence-meaning, negation, and Plato's problem of Non-being', in G. Vlastos (ed.), *Plato*, vol. 1, 1971.

INDEXES

1. INDEX OF REFERENCES TO PASSAGES OF PLATO

(References to the *Sophist* itself are not included in this index.)

2. INDEX OF GREEK TERMS

3. GENERAL INDEX